ASPECTS IN

VEDIC ASTROLOGY

*Other Passage Press Books by Pandit Gopesh Kumar Ojha
and Pandit Ashutosh Ojha*

LOVE AND MARRIAGE IN VEDIC ASTROLOGY
(Forthcoming)

PRACTICAL ASTROLOGY OF THE HINDUS
(Forthcoming)

THE SOLAR RETURN
(Forthcoming)

VEDIC PHYSIOGNOMY
(Forthcoming)

ASPECTS IN

VEDIC ASTROLOGY

by Pandit Gopesh Kumar Ojha
and Pandit Ashutosh Ojha

Edited by Kenneth Johnson

Passage Press
Salt Lake City, Utah

Passage Press is a division of Morson Publishing
Morson Publishing
P.O. Box 21713
Salt Lake City, Utah 84121-0713

Published 1992

Printed in the United States of America

Cover design by Ted Nagata

Printed on acid-free paper

ISBN 1-878423-15-0

CONTENTS

INTRODUCTION

The science of the heavens is broadly divided into two branches — astronomy and astrology. Astrology itself has many branches — mundane astrology, which deals with rains, meteorology, crops, storms, floods and droughts, fires, volcanic eruptions, seismic disturbances, natural calamities and disasters, etc.; political astrology, dealing with the rise and fall of nations, kings and empires, riots, wars, changes of government and the like; commercial astrology, involving the rise and fall of prices, scarcity or abundance of commodities, inflation or deflation in stocks and shares, bullion, food, famine and pestilence; electional astrology, which deals with the selection of the appropriate time for commencement or consummation of a particular work of importance; and natal astrology, pertaining to birth times and nativities. Then there is horary astrology and the system of annual solar returns, solar ingresses, monthly solar returns, lunar returns, daily returns and a vast astrological literature on transits. Even in natal astrology there are three branches: esoteric astrology deals with the question "why," while directions, transits, mahadashas and antardashas (called bhuktis in South India), along with many other methods, address the intricate and complex problem of "when." Parashara, the father of Hindu astrology, discusses forty-three kinds of mahadashas and Jaimini, another old master, about a dozen. There is a vast literature on the subject. But the basic principle in the Western as well as the Hindu system is that only those things come to pass which are ordained in the radix (the birth chart and the root of all predictions), and scholars all over the world, in the past as well as in the present, have devoted much time, energy and experience to the question of "what" in the context of natal astrology. Even this "what" is not easy or simple to define. It embraces signs and subdivisions, the Ascendant and the other houses, and planets — their state, strength and modalities, various planetary patterns (called yogas in Hindu astrology), conjunctions and aspects, etc. Our experience, which is shared by many astrologers, has been that the "when" in astrology is based on calculations which, though involving protracted time and energy, are made easy due to their conforming to mathematical processes, but the "what" requires a delicate balancing of, at times, paradoxical indications, and it is to help in this balancing that the conjunctions and aspects prove a helpful and reliable guide.

In Western astrology most textbooks deal with conjunctions and aspects along with other matters. Mr. C. E. O. Carter, in addition to writing several books such as *The Principles of Astrology* and *Some Principles of Horoscopic Astrological Delineation*, also thought fit to write a whole book entitled *The Astrological Aspects,* devoted exclusively to the conjunctions and aspects of planets. According to this late celebrated British astrologer (and many would share his conviction, as we do), the conjunctions and aspects play a pivotal role in the matter of predictions. And yet we have not come across any book dealing exclusively with the subject from the point of view of Hindu astrology. True, the standard works written in Sanskrit during the ancient and medieval periods touch on the matter, but the guidelines are scarce and scattered. And it is with a view to filling this void that we have, in this book, condensed the cream of knowledge collected from about twenty standard Sanskrit works of outstanding authority and repute.

A book dealing with the subject according to the canons of Hindu astrology is not a luxury but a necessity, for more reasons than one. First, a larger and larger number of astrologers in the West, professional as well as amateur, are taking an interest in Hindu astrology. Second, even for Indian scholars there is no single book dealing with the subject in such detail. In the Hindu and Western systems there are some fundamental differences in approach to the subject. Most Western books delineate evil effects for square and opposition aspects, except Mr. Carter, who states that "inharmonious aspects cause misfortunes but they do not forbid success." Similarly most of the Western writers from the Middle Ages onward have called trines and sextiles good. But Mr. Carter makes an exception here also, and calls these aspects inharmonious if the planets involved are of contrary nature. In Hindu astrology, however, as readers will observe, the criteria are quite different. Astrologers following the Hindu system have available a large literature in English to supplement their own knowledge with that of the West, but there is no detailed book in English projecting the fundamental image of Hindu astrology in the matter of aspects.

With this in view, the present book has been written, and we have picked and chosen out of what the old masters wrote in Sanskrit and what has been reinforced by our own experiences during forty-eight years of astrological practice. If readers will bestow their attention upon the precepts in this guide, our efforts will be amply rewarded.

Our effort has been not just to collect gems from the old masters and string them together, but to offer our comments and criticism at every relevant stage to help our readers to better understand and appreciate the astrological significance of particular aspects. The cardinal principles provided by the conjunctions and aspects are valuable for general appraisal as well. And if we have invited attention to a particular feature at more than one place, it has been to emphasize it so that the readers may better assimilate it.

It must be added, for the guidance of our Western readers, that Hindu astrology is based on the sidereal zodiac, and that the tropical longitudes of the Ascendant and the planets must be converted into sidereal ones for appraisal of the influence of conjunctions and aspects as given in this book.

How to make the conversion? Take the longitudes of planets as given in the tropical zodiac and deduct the correction for the precession of the equinoxes on the date of birth from the tropical longitude of each planet. The correction for precession on January 1st of the following years was as follows:

1900	22° 27' 59"
1910	22° 35' 51"
1920	22° 44' 43"
1930	22° 52' 40"
1940	23° 01' 21"
1950	23° 09' 34"
1960	23° 17' 54"
1970	23° 26' 21"
1980	23° 34' 31"
1990	23° 42' 56"

The correction for the years in between can be worked out by adding 48 seconds per year; the approximate value will be found. Why approximate? Because the rate is not strictly uniform.

The value of precession should also be deducted from the longitude of the Ascendant or First house cusp. Once the sidereal sign on the cusp of the First house is ascertained, the other houses follow in the regular order of the signs. If, for instance, sidereal Sagittarius is on the cusp of the First house, the whole sign of Sagittarius would constitute the First house, the sign of Capricorn the Second, the entire thirty degrees of Aquarius the Third and so on. We will discuss this point in Chapter 10, but it is necessary to invite attention to it at the initial stage so that Western readers accustomed to the tropical zodiac and the Western systems of houses do not begin on wrong premises.

In interpreting astrological factors, it is necessary to keep in mind the general background and environment of the native. Jupiter is in one sign for about a year and Saturn for two and a half years, so that all children born during a particular twelve-month period will have the same Jupiter-Saturn conjunction if one occurred that year. So while the basic effect would be common to a large number of people, the details may be modified according to other factors as discussed in the final chapter. Also, heredity and environment will play a large roll. As one's society is structured, certain careers may be denied to women, and even where a particular avenue is open to both sexes, the women may be at a certain disadvantage due to other social and biological factors. But when these handicaps are absent, and if women were to follow a particular career in agriculture, commerce, education or politics, the same effects would manifest themselves regardless of the native's sex.

While assessing astrological influences, we have used the expression "the native" or "he" but, as in law, "he" includes "she" and the descriptions can be applied mutatis mutandis to women also. But expressions such as "hairy body," "fondness for damsels," and "liaisons with others' wives" will naturally have a different interpretation in the context of female nativities. Nor can characteristics such as "black eyes" apply universally to people of all countries and ethnic origins. Or to take another example, owning a conveyance or a car or cars would appear to be of no great significance to a citizen of a country where almost everyone owns a car, but would be quite significant in India, where the masses suffer from privation and penury. The art of interpretation, therefore, rests with the astrologer, who must take cognizance of times, places, heredity and environment.

As far as the traits of character and temperament are concerned, they should be applied to both sexes alike, but we would like to issue a note of warning that readers should exercise restraint and circumspection in pronouncing judgment on the moral delinquencies of women. First, there may be other astrological factors nullifying or modifying a particular feature. Second, Indian society has different moral values and flirtation is not as common there as it is in the West. Also, due to a particular configuration of planets, the heart may be inclined to certain erratic tendencies but the mind may restrain the native so that there is no overt action. So our readers should rather abstain from pronouncement on such delicate matters lest they unwittingly shatter the domestic happiness of a married woman or the prospects of a marriageable girl.

A word is necessary in regard to the use of "he" or "she" in relation to the planets. Western astrologers use "she" for the Moon and Venus, and "he" for the others. According to Hindu astrology as well, the Sun, Mars and Jupiter are masculine in influence, while the Moon and Venus are feminine. Mercury is described as a "female eunuch" and Saturn as a "male eunuch." But as regards the planets in the mythological texts and in paintings from old, all seven planets are referred to as "he" and portrayed as males. There is a mythological story that the Moon had a liaison with Jupiter's wife Tara and that Mercury was born of this union. According to another myth, Venus (called Shukra or Ushanas in Sanskrit) acted as a priest to King Bali. Shukra had two wives — Jayanti, daughter of Indra, and Go, daughter of the Manes. Shukra had four sons — Twastra, Varutrin, Shanda and Marka — by his wives. Orthodox Brahmins offer prayers every day to the nine planets and refer to all of them as "he," and in the old texts only the masculine gender is used for them. Under the circumstances we have used "he" for the Moon and Venus also. We have done so in other published works as well.

In Hindu astrology only nine planets are recognized — the Sun, the Moon, Mars, Mercury, Jupiter, Venus, Saturn, Rahu and Ketu. No cognizance is taken of the trans-Saturnian planets — Uranus, Neptune, and Pluto, or any other planets that may be discovered hereafter. Strictly speaking, the Sun and Moon are luminaries, but for convenience they are also referred to as planets in astrological parlance. Rahu and Ketu are the North and South Nodes of the Moon and they are accorded more importance in Hindu astrology than in Western. But the Nodes are merely sensitive points; they have no body, no mass, no weight. They do not aspect nor are they aspected. The North Node of the Moon, the Caput Draconis, is the head (represented in Hindu paintings as the head of a demon without the trunk), and the South Node of the Moon, the Cauda Draconis (represented as the body without the head), is the tail. Some older texts have argued that the head, having eyes, must cast aspects, and have thus assigned some aspects to Caput Draconis. But this logic is fallacious. The planets aspect with their hind parts as animals do. Besides, everything in astrology cannot be explained on the basis of reasoning alone. There are mystic depths which are difficult to probe. To revert to the Nodes, though here and there we come across references to conjunctions with or aspects to Rahu in some texts, the standard view is that the Nodes are shadows and imbibe the characteristics of the house and sign they are in or of the planets with which they are conjoined. Therefore the older masters have not dealt with Rahu or Ketu's conjunctions and aspects.

One other point is worthy of mention. Western astrologers have deemed Caput Draconis as benefic and Cauda Draconis as malefic. But in Hindu astrology the North Node is treated like Saturn and the South like Mars — in short, they are both malefic. However, for judging their effect, these planets are deemed well posited in the Third, Sixth or

Eleventh houses. Also, if a Node is in an angle and conjunct the lord of a trine house[1] or if it tenants a trine house and conjoins the lord of an angle,[2] it is treated as excellent. Though the Nodes do not aspect nor are they aspected, a special corollary arises in the latter case. Let us say that Caput Draconis is in Aries and Jupiter in Sagittarius. Granting that Caput Draconis is not aspected by Jupiter, we have to admit that Jupiter aspects Aries, and as a result of this aspect by a strong benefic the general qualities of Aries are improved with the result that even the Node tenanting this sign shares the good resulting from Jupiter's aspect.

We have dealt with conjunctions of planets in the first three chapters and aspects in the next three. But in Hindu astrology the Ninth house is deemed the most important. It is the house of luck and prosperity, and also of religious merit. The First, Fifth and Ninth constitute a trine; but if the First house is allotted one unit of goodness, the Fifth house is assigned two and the Ninth three. Standard astrological texts state that the Eighth house is the worst because it is the twelfth (loss, expenditure) from the Ninth (good luck) and nothing can be so evil as loss of good luck, and when the fruit of religious merit is exhausted life comes to an end. Others opine that the Eighth is the house of death because it symbolizes loss (twelfth) of religious merit. Be that as it may, we have, in the tradition of a medieval author, devoted a whole chapter to conjunctions in the Ninth house, also dealing extensively with Jupiter in that house and aspected by various planets singly and collectively. Therefore, though in earlier chapters there are scattered references to conjunctions in the Ninth house, a methodical treatment has been reserved for a separate chapter.

This book deals with the aspects of one planet on another, but we have not dealt with the aspects of planets to the Ascendant for the simple reason that Varaha Mihira in the *Brihat Jataka,* Chapter 18, verse 20, states:

> "The results which have been stated for the presence of the Moon in each sign and the results of the aspects of other planets on the Moon should be applied to aspects on the Ascendant also."

---

1   The trine houses are the First, Fifth and Ninth. They are auspicious or favorable by nature.
2   The angles or angular houses are the First, Fourth, Seventh and Tenth, the most innately powerful of all the houses.

Thus if the Ascendant is, say, Aries and is aspected by Jupiter, there will be the same effect as when Jupiter aspects the Moon in Aries.

It is important to invite the attention of the readers to one point. This volume does not supplant our other book, *Predictive Astrology of the Hindus*[3], but only supplements it. We have taken care not to reiterate here what we have stated about the conjunctions and aspects of planets in that book, and those who want to master the subject should derive fuller benefit if they peruse that book and learn about the effect of individual planets in the various houses and signs, and in particular in special degrees of each sign. That book will also familiarize readers with the vivid contours of predictive astrology as propounded and practiced by the Hindus.

We have, in the penultimate chapter, given chosen aphorisms from the standard Sanskrit texts and then in the last chapter provided broad guidelines for appraisal which will be found useful not only for better understanding and appreciation of the matters dealt with in this book, but for astrological judgment in general and Hindu astrology in particular.

---

3   Ojha, Pandit Gopesh Kumar. *Predictive Astrology of the Hindus,* Bombay, D. B. Taraporevala Sons & Co., 1990. Available in the United States through Passage Press.

1
CONJUNCTIONS
OF TWO PLANETS

In Western astrology the conjunction of two planets is one of the aspects, like the trine, square or opposition. Not so in Hindu astrology. Here the conjunction of one or more planets produces an effect which, at times, is different from that caused by an aspect.

What is a conjunction? It means the conjoining of two or more planets. In Western astrology two planets (be they in the same or adjoining signs) are deemed in conjunction if they are within a specified distance from each other. If two planets are at exactly the same degree it is a perfect conjunction, but that rarely happens. The distance between two planets is called the orb, and planets are treated as conjunct despite a distance of a few degrees intervening between them. In Western astrology the orbs allowed between the various planets for purposes of conjunction are a topic of lively debate, but a standard barometer may be outlined as follows:

1. The orb of the planets when applying should be six degrees, and, when separating, eight degrees in the case of Mars, Mercury, Jupiter, Venus and Saturn.

2. The orb of the Sun when applying may be taken as twelve degrees and, when separating, as seventeen degrees.

3. The orb of the Moon when applying may be taken as eight degrees, and when separating as twelve degrees.

But this is Western astrology. In Hindu astrology, if the two planets are in the same sign they are treated as being in conjunction, even if one is in the first degree of the sign and the other in the thirtieth degree. But if they are in different signs (even though the intervening distance between them be only four or five degrees) they are not treated as conjunct.

It must always be remembered that signs, as referred to above or anywhere else in this book, means the sign in the *sidereal* zodiac and not the tropical zodiac. If two planets are in the same tropical sign but in different sidereal signs they should not be regarded as conjunct. Conversely, if two planets are in the same sidereal sign but in different tropical signs, they will be deemed conjunct.

✳ ✳ ✳

CONJUNCTIONS OF THE SUN

Sun and Moon

If the Sun and Moon are together, the native will be gifted in mechanics and may gain money by manufacturing machinery and parts, and also by dealing in wares made of stone. He will be clever in his work, and may gain by trading in spirits and liqueurs or fermented drugs. He will be diplomatic in his dealings and very rich, but will be under the influence of his spouse or the opposite sex.

If the Sun and Moon are conjoined in the Ascendant, the native suffers in regard to both parents. He may be prematurely separated from them or may not receive his due love and affection from them. He commands respect in society but does not accumulate much wealth and also suffers in respect to children. He suffers humiliation and is not happy.

If the two luminaries conjoin in the Fourth house, the native is devoid of good relations and sons, is unintelligent and poor.

If the two luminaries conjoin in the Seventh house, the native is devoid of friends and sons and is always humiliated by members of the opposite sex or frustrated in respect to or through desire for them.

If the Sun and Moon are together in the Tenth, the native has a good body; he is famous and is the leader of many people, will suppress his enemies, will be cruel and of uneven temper. He will be acquisitive and gather much paraphernalia.

According to the *Horasara*, if the two luminaries are in the Ninth the native is rich; if they are in the Twelfth he may be blind or may suffer in respect to eyesight. Except in the Ninth, this combination is generally not conducive to wealth unless the Moon is within 12° of the Sun, in which case the native is rich and famous.

Sun and Mars

If the Sun and Mars are together the native is sinful (i.e. cruel in his actions). He is not truthful in speech but has strength and stamina and a forceful personality. He does not exercise his discretion properly.

If the two planets are together in the Ascendant the native suffers from bilious ailments.[1] He is of fiery temper, wicked in his intentions, cruel in his deeds and hard-hearted, but he fights his opponents with daring and fortitude. He may have scars on his body or suffer a fracture of the bone.

If the two planets are in the Fourth, the native is devoid of good relations and wealth. He is always dissatisfied and frustrated; he has no happiness and scant comfort. He is envied by people; he himself is envious.

A conjunction of the Sun and Mars in the Fourth house will be good rather than difficult if Leo is the Ascendant, for in such a case it will be a conjunction of the lords of the First, Fourth and Ninth houses. The *Jatakalankar,* Chapter 1, verse 9, states that if the lord of the Fourth is in his own house and conjunct the lord of the First there will be a sudden gain of immovable property (i.e. real estate).

If the two planets are in the Seventh, the native suffers sorrow due to separation from his spouse and humiliation on account of the opposite sex (he may be let down by them or his desires frustrated). He is inclined to travel in foreign countries.

If the two planets are in the Tenth, the native occupies a high government post, but is restless in disposition and always agitated, and projects undertaken by him remain unfulfilled.

The *Horasara* states that if the combination of the Sun and Mars occurs in the First, Eighth, Tenth or Eleventh house, the native will be born in an upstanding family and will be strong, but if it is found in a house other than those listed above the native will be poor.

Sun and Mercury

If the Sun and Mercury are together the native is intelligent and efficient in the execution of his work; he is happy and earns both name

---

1   In Hindu astrology, medical problems are classified according to Ayurveda, the traditional or yogic medicine of India. Ayurveda recognizes three human constitutions or doshas, governed by the five elements: Vata (air/ether, also known as wind), Pitta (fire/water, also called bile), and Kapha (earth/water or phlegm). The above example refers to problems caused by an imbalance of Pitta and typified by "fiery" characteristics, such as headaches, fevers, inflammation or high blood pressure.

and fame. He has strength and fixity of mind and a good appearance. The native follows a career of service, is liked by his superiors and is wealthy, but his finances fluctuate. According to the *Horasara*, if Mercury and the Sun are conjoined in the Fourth or Eighth from the Ascendant it constitues a rajayoga[2] for wealth and position. In other houses, it acts as a moderately good influence.

If the two planets are conjoined in the First house the individual is intelligent, eloquent and learned. He has a solid body and is long-lived.

The two planets in the Fourth make him very wealthy; he has a good constitution, occupies a high position and is learned.

If the Sun and Mercury are in the Seventh, the native meets an unnatural death; he accepts the advice of others and is not avaricious but has thievish tendencies. He does not have much marital happiness.

If the two planets are in the Tenth, the native has many material goods, is very famous and occupies a lordly position. But the above good effects do not fructify if the conjunction takes place in Libra or Pisces, i.e. the signs in which either of the two planets would be debilitated.

Sun and Jupiter

If the Sun and Jupiter are conjoined together, the native is cruel at heart and engages in other people's work. He will have good faith (in religion), will be wealthy, and his actions will win the approbation of his master. He gains from his friends and may engage in the profession of teaching.

If the Sun and Jupiter are together in the First, the native has many admirable qualities and may become the head of an institution with a large staff working under him. If other combinations agree, he may also become an ascetic. The native is learned, rich and famous; he has extensive luxuries.

If the two planets are in the Fourth, the native is given to learning and is fond of poetry and scriptures. He has a good personality and is sweet to talk to. He is rich, but his mode of conduct is concealed.

If the above planets are in the Seventh, the native is antagonistic to his father. He has a good personality and is rich but, due to a strong amorous disposition, he is completely under the influence of his wife.

---

2 This is a Sanskrit word, literally meaning "royal combination," and is used to indicate a configuration of planets which causes high rank and position and confers riches.

If the Sun and Jupiter are in the Tenth, the native attains an elevated position in life, even if he is born into a "low" family. He enjoys a comfortable living, is wealthy, and earns respect, name and fame for himself.

The *Horasara* states that if a Sun-Jupiter conjunction occurs in the First, Ninth, Tenth or Eleventh house, the native will have a large band of people at his command and will be famous.

Sun and Venus

If the Sun and Venus are conjunct the native earns money by dealing in things having to do with the eyes, colors, paints, or from the stage, theater, cinema, public amusements, weapons, arms and ammunition. The native will be intelligent. There may be gain through the wife or her relations, or from other contacts due to ladies. The native may also be efficient in the use of arms, but his eyesight is impaired if the two planets are in the Twelfth, Second, Sixth or Eighth.

If the Sun and Venus are together in the First, the native is a little rough in his manners. His conduct is not free from blemish; he may resort to low acts and is unhappy. The native is argumentative and prone to quarreling. On account of his intensely amorous inclinations, he may even leave his marriage partner.

If the combination occurs in the Fourth house, the native serves others and is not wealthy; he is sad and melancholy and envied by others.

If the two planets are in the Seventh, the native has a large body and is envied by others. He is fond of roaming in hills and forests. He suffers humiliation at the hands of the opposite sex.

If the planets are in the Tenth, the native will occupy an exalted position. He will be intelligent, learned and clever in dealing with others. He will be wealthy, have conveyances, and lead a comfortable life.

The *Horasara* states that if the Sun and Venus are together in the Fifth, Eighth or Tenth house, the native will be famous and lead a kingly life. In other houses, the conjunction makes one poor.

Sun and Saturn

If the Sun and Saturn are together, the native is clever in dealing in pottery, metals, alloys or articles made from metals and alloys. He will not be very intelligent and will be oppressed by his enemies. There is likelihood of the premature death of a son or consort. The native has a religious bent of mind and follows the tradition of his family but does not have an even temper.

If the two planets are in the First house, the native's conduct is not good, his inclinations are not pious, and his mother may have suffered some disrespect.

If the combination occurs in the Fourth house, the native's conduct is low; he is oppressed by his relations and leads an indigent life.

If the two planets are in the Seventh, the native is slow and indolent. He is bereft of wealth and consort. There may be premature separation from the marriage partner. Such a person is fond of hunting and dull-witted or unwise in his actions.

If the combination is in the Tenth house, the native follows a career of service and lives abroad in a country other than his homeland. At times he derives good income from his employers, but he is likely to lose his wealth due to theft.

The *Horasara* states that if the conjunction occurs in the Second, Sixth or Ninth house, the native will be happy and famous, but in other houses it makes one poor. Some sources say that this combination in the Second is indicative of poverty rather than wealth.

CONJUNCTIONS OF THE MOON

Moon and Mars

If the Moon and Mars are together it is a good combination for riches but unfavorable for mothers. The native is diplomatic and courageous. He may gain from alloys, spirits and liquors, and also from merchandise or articles made of clay or leather or things noted for artisanship. He may suffer from some disease arising out of deficiency, impurity, or poor circulation of the blood.

If the Moon and Mars are together in the First house, the native is short tempered but attains a high position. He suffers from bilious diseases[3] or those pertaining to the blood. He may also suffer from fire or injury to the head.

If the two planets are in the Fourth, the native has a restless disposition. He has no peace of mind. He is devoid of good relations, wealth and happiness. This is detrimental to sons also.

If the combination is in the Seventh house, the native is mean, envious and avaricious of others' wealth. He speaks much but his speech is not truthful.

---

3   See footnote on Ayurveda, p. 17.

When the two planets are in the Tenth, the native is very valorous. He has a number of vehicles and possesses many luxury items. He is wealthy.

The *Horasara* states that if the conjunction of the Moon and Mars occurs in the Ascendant, the Fifth, Ninth, Tenth or Eleventh house, the native is very wealthy, like a king, but if the conjunction is in a house other than those mentioned above he is devoid of good relations and happiness.

Moon and Mercury

If the Moon and Mercury are together, the native is religious, learned, and has many merits. He has a literary turn of mind and is rich. He has a smiling face, is jocular, and is liked by ladies. The native's speech is good; it is not overbearing. He leads a prosperous life and becomes famous.

If the combination occurs in the First house he has intelligence and stamina. He has a comely appearance, is eloquent, and very clever in his work.

If the two planets are in the Fourth, the native has an attractive appearance, is very wealthy, endowed with vehicles, and has good children, friends and relations.

If the Moon and Mercury are in the Seventh, he is poetic and has well-developed aesthetic tastes. The native attains a high position and is liked by his superiors. He becomes famous.

If the two planets are in the Tenth house, the native is proud, wealthy and very famous. He rises to a high position in life, but in his old age he is abandoned by his relations and becomes sorrowful.

The *Horasara* states that when the combination of the Moon and Mercury occurs in the Third, Sixth, Eighth or Twelfth house, the native will have a literary and poetic turn of mind and will be wealthy. In houses other than those listed above, the native will be fearless but poor.

Moon and Jupiter

The conjunction of the Moon and Jupiter is a very good one. The native is courageous, very wealthy, the head of his clan, and of fixed determination. He is very intelligent and has the company of good people. Also, he does good to them and gives due respect to his kinsmen. His friendship is fast and he is gentle and courteous.

If the two planets are in the First house, the native has a broad elevated chest. He rises high in life and occupies an eminent position. He has a good body and good relations. He is happy as regards wife, sons and friends.

If the combination occurs in the Fourth house, the native may rise to the position of a minister. He has many luxury goods. He is intelligent and learned and leads a happy and comfortable life. He is endowed with happiness in respect to his relations.

If the two planets are in the Seventh house, the native is intelligent, clever, a favorite of the king and wealthy. He engages in trade and commerce and rises to a high position.

If the Moon and Jupiter are in the Tenth, the native has long arms. He is cool-headed and good-looking. He is learned and wealthy and commands respect. He is also bountiful in giving.

Moon and Venus

If the Moon and Venus are together, the native is clever in the purchase and sale of cloth. He may be generally clever in trade and merchandise, but he is also likely to be evil-minded. He puts on fine apparel and is fond of scents and flowers. He is liked by his people and clever in the execution of his work, but he is indolent. According to the *Horasara*, if the combination occurs in the Twelfth house there is gain of money from foreign lands.

If the combination is in the First house, the native is fond of fine apparel, scents and flowers. He has a pleasing personality and is a favorite of his seniors. He derives much pleasure from the company of dancing girls.

If the two planets conjoin in the Fourth house, the native is popular. He has all the paraphernalia of luxury. He gains financially from ships, boats, or from articles transported by or across water. He has much happiness as regards the opposite sex.

If the Moon and Venus combine in the Seventh house, the native is intelligent but not very wealthy. He may enter government service. He will be attached to several women and have few sons but several daughters.

When the conjunction of these two planets is in the Tenth house, the native is of a forgiving disposition. He has a number of people around him and may be a famous minister or even a king. He commands respect and is obeyed. He is wealthy.

Moon and Saturn

If the Moon and Saturn are together, the native's mother may have remarried. The native does not have good relations with his spouse; he will be a source of unhappiness to his father. He will be devoid of wealth and subordinate to another; he will have liaisons with women older than himself. He will be well versed in training horses and elephants. If engaged in strife or controversy, he will be vanquished by his opponent.

If the combination occurs in the First house, the native is sinful, sleepy, indolent, avaricious and wicked. He is discourteous and spends his life in a subordinate position.

If the two planets are in the Fourth house, the native earns money by digging (or from products taken out of the bowels of the earth). He may also earn from water transport, pearls, jewels or articles transported by or across water. He becomes powerful and popular.

If the conjunction is in the Seventh house, the native occupies a high position in his village or town and is respected by the government. But he suffers in respect to his spouse or through marital happiness.

If the combination occurs in the Tenth house, the native subdues his enemies, is famous, and becomes the head of a large number of men, but his relationship with his mother is not good.

According to the *Horasara*, if the Moon and Saturn are conjunct the native has a weak body, resorts to low acts, is dull-witted and antagonistic to his mother, but if the conjunction is in the Third, Sixth, Tenth or Eleventh house, he is wealthy. In the Fifth it will promote studies which require depth of thought. Our experience is that the Moon-Saturn conjunction makes one thoughtful and pessimistic and, unless benefics aspect this conjunction, the native is likely to be moody and melancholy.

CONJUNCTIONS OF MARS

Mars and Mercury

If Mars and Mercury conjoin, the native may gain by trade and commerce. Dealing in plants, timber, trees, and all oily or greasy substances will be particularly gainful. He may also benefit from diplomatic speech. He will have strong arms and can be a good wrestler. The native is eloquent and can gain from the sale or practice of medicine, arts, crafts, and working with machinery parts requiring ingenuity. The manufacture or sale of gold ornaments would also suit him. But the native is not very rich and does not have a good marriage. He may have liaisons with wicked women or widows. According to the *Horasara*, the native is very active but uncouth, and wants to live at the expense of others. He is satisfied with ordinary riches. But if the conjuncton occurs in an angle from the Ascendant, the native is rich and leads a comfortable life.

If the two planets conjoin in the Ascendant, the native is cruel and aggressive, efficient in work where fire is used; he gains in the manufacture of metal articles; he may be a good ambassador. He can also do well in the secret service.

If the two planets combine in the Fourth house, the native is devoid of good relations or may be boycotted by them, but he has friends. He is possessed of wealth and property and leads a comfortable life.

If the conjunction occurs in the Seventh, the native wanders from place to place and is oppressed by low people. He is very argumentative and enters into controversies. His first marriage partner dies prematurely.

If the two planets combine in the Tenth house, the native is bold and persevering. He is liked by the king. He will be cruel and wicked and may become the head of a section of the army or occupy some other equally important post.

Mars and Jupiter

If Mars and Jupiter are together, the native becomes the mayor of a town or if he is a Brahmin[4] he may receive money and patronage from the king. The native will be proficient in mathematics. He will have many meritorious qualities but will be over-sexed. The general consensus is that the native will be learned, well up in the arts and crafts, intelligent and eloquent and well versed in the use of weapons. He will be strong, courteous, have sons and a long life; but, according to the *Horasara,* if the conjunction occurs in the Sixth, Eighth or Twelfth house the native will be addicted to some vice and will be sickly and poor.

If Mars and Jupiter conjoin in the First house, the native is always very enthusiastic. He will have many admirable qualities and will earn fame in the religious field. He may become the minister of a king or occupy some other equally eminent post.

If the conjunction occurs in the Fourth house, the native will be of fixed determination and lead a comfortable life. He will have friends and good relations. He will be devoted to the gods and his religious preceptors. He will occupy a good post under the king.

If the two planets combine in the Seventh house, the native is fond of roaming in mountains, forests, and watery places (the riverside or seaside). He is very courageous. He has good relations but is without a spouse or marital happiness.

If Mars and Jupiter combine in the Tenth house, the native attains a kingly position and enjoys much fame. He is very capable; he has much wealth and a large family.

---

4   The priestly caste among Hindus.

Mars and Venus

If Mars and Venus conjoin, the native is fond of betting, gambling or speculation. He may have a large herd of cows. He may be a strong wrestler and a very capable person in most respects, but he is attached to other people's wives. The native may be very efficient in metallurgy but is of a scheming nature and cunning. He will have a respectable position and may be an important member of his clan. He may also be skilled in mathematics, but his inherent nature is wicked. According to the *Horasara,* the person will be rash, under the influence of his spouse (or someone of the opposite sex), and his acts will be vicious; but if the conjunction occurs in the First, Fourth or Tenth house, he will rise above his station in life and become a leader.

When the two planets are together in the Ascendant, the native is not long-lived. His conduct is not good. He wastes his wealth on the opposite sex and is attached to people of loose morals.

If the two planets conjoin in the Fourth house, the native suffers from constant mental anguish. He is oppressed by various calamities. He has no happiness from children, relations or friends. Mark the difference between this statement and the one in the *Horasara.* The native may be rich or have a good position but he does not have happiness.

When Mars and Venus combine in the Seventh, the native is constantly tempted to indulge in numerous sexual affairs. His character is not good. He meets with great sorrow and anguish of mind due to the opposite sex.

When the conjunction occurs in the Tenth house, the native is well-versed in the use of weapons; he is very intelligent and learned. He is wealthy and has plenty of enjoyment; he leads a life of luxury. He attains fame and occupies a very high rank.

We have observed that Mars and Venus together always make one's sex life unsatisfactory. Mars represents the urge of erotic passions in a female, while Venus is symbolic of lust in a male. When the two planets combine in a nativity, the psychology of sex becomes abnormal and married life is seldom satisfactory.

Mars and Saturn

When Mars and Saturn are together the native commits acts of infamy. He is not truthful and suffers from mental anguish. According to the *Jataka Parijata,* the native will be contentious but not intelligent. He will, however, be a connoisseur of music and drama (particularly farce). According to Kalyan Varma he will be irreligious, quarrelsome, and will have a tendency to practice deception on others. He will have a thievish disposition. He will be clever in metallurgy and in creating an atmosphere which, though unreal, will have a semblance of reality (as is done with silver and gold-plated articles or by jugglers or in circus shows). According to the *Horasara* the native suffers from diseases arising out of bile and wind[5] and also suffers mentally or physically from a chronic disease, but if the conjunction takes place in the Third, Sixth, Tenth or Eleventh house from the Ascendant he will attain a high position, will be popular and famous. According to the *Jataka Parijata,* Mars and Saturn together in the Second may cause various diseases.

If the above two planets are in the Ascendant the native is not long-lived. His prosperity is at a low ebb. He does not have cordial relations with his mother. But he is victorious in contest, strife or warfare. We believe that the above effects, described in an ancient text, do not apply if the sign Capricorn is rising.

If the conjunction takes place in the Fourth, the native will be abandoned or boycotted by his relations. He will be sinful in his acts, devoid of friends and happiness. His life will not be one of comfort.

If Mars and Saturn are together in the Seventh, the native is miserly and oppressed by other people. He is sickly, addicted to vices, and leads a humble life. He has no happiness either in respect to his married life or children.

Mantreshwar, the highly regarded author of the *Phala Deepika*, an authoritative medieval work in Sanskrit on predictive astrology, makes an exception; if Mars and Saturn are together in Cancer in the Seventh house the native's spouse will be chaste and attractive.

When the two planets combine in the Tenth, the native gains much money from the government but is also punished by the government for a major offense. The native is not truthful.

CONJUNCTIONS OF MERCURY

Mercury and Jupiter

According to Varaha Mihira, when Mercury and Jupiter are together the individual is fond of songs, music and dance. If other indications agree, he may excel in dance, drama, acting, etc. The native will have a pleasing personality, be of good speech and have many merits. He will be very rich. These two benefics together make one wise and intelligent; he leads a comfortable life. According to the *Horasara* the native is no doubt

---

5   i.e. Pitta and Vata; see Ayurveda footnote, p. 17.

learned, but his eyesight suffers; he may also develop deafness. But if the conjunction takes place in either the Sixth, Eighth or Twelfth house he will be of comely appearance and famous in the religious field.

If the two planets conjoin in the First, the native is endowed with all kinds of comforts, conveyances, and articles of luxury. He has a pleasing personality. He is courteous, well behaved and learned. He is respected by the king.

If the conjunction takes place in the Fourth, the native has wealth and conjugal happiness. He has good friends and relations and leads a happy life. He is clever and is liked by the king.

If the two planets are in the Seventh, the native has a good marriage partner; he has great stamina and conquers his enemies. He has a large number of friends and is wealthy. He rises far above the status of his father.

If Mercury and Jupiter are in the Tenth, the native may become a king or a king's minister (in a modern context, this would be interpreted as occupying a high position). He is courteous and well mannered. He commands much respect and his orders are obeyed. He is religious in outlook and his actions are good.

Mercury and Venus

If Mercury and Venus are together, the native is learned, eloquent and clever in dealing with others. He becomes a leader among land owners or trade unions. If both Mercury and Venus are strong, the native may occupy a very high position in life. Mercury stands for intelligence and Venus for art. A combination of the two makes one fond of art and mirth. The native is diplomatic and very wealthy. He is also clever in arts and crafts. His aesthetic sense is highly developed. According to the *Horasara*, this combination makes one restless. The native can mount a successful offensive, but has little happiness from marriage or children. But if the two planets are in either the First, Fifth or Ninth house, he will be very wealthy and famous.

Let us now examine the effects of the two planets together in the angles. When they are in the First house, the native has a handsome and attractive personality. He will be much respected and will be a favorite of the king.

When the conjunction is in the Fourth, the native has a comely face and figure. He has good relations, children and friends; he has worldly prosperity and occupies a high rank.

When the two planets are in the Seventh, the native is surrounded by a large number of beautiful damsels. He is happy, leads a luxurious life and is liked by the king.

When the conjunction takes place in the Tenth, the native is very diplomatic. He is capable and his projects are successful. He is quite rich and may occupy a very high position. He patronizes only good people.

Mercury and Saturn

If Mercury and Saturn are together, the native is clever in deceiving others. He has a tendency to transgress moral and social laws. Mercury is intelligence; Saturn is depth. This depth can be used in worldly matters, i.e. in hiding one's own thoughts and thus practicing deception. In highly intelligent and scrupulous people this depth may be used to better purpose, such as deep and profound study of philosophy and the sciences. But an affliction of both the Moon and Mercury by Saturn at times leads to neurosis, derangement of the brain, or lunacy.

According to the *Horasara*, if Mercury and Saturn conjoin in either the First, Ninth or Tenth house, the native is wealthy; he has a spouse, children and friends (i.e. happiness in respect to them), but if they conjoin in any other house the effect is mostly evil. According to the *Jataka Parijata*, the native will be religious and wealthy and will be a person of merit. But Kalyan Varma does not think highly of this combination: he states that the native speaks sweetly and is clever but runs into debts, has a tendency to deceive others and is a hypocrite.

When Mercury and Saturn are in the First, the native has an uncouth body and lacks a good education, wealth and conveyances. His actions are sinful. He is not fortunate and has a short life.

When these planets are in the Fourth, the native's actions are not commendable. He has no good friends or relations. His people forsake him. He does not lead a comfortable life.

When the conjunction takes place in the Seventh, the native has an unclean appearance. He is not truthful nor is his conduct good. He is dull-witted and does not do good to others. He may be in the employment of others.

When the two planets combine in the Tenth, the native vanquishes all his enemies; he has his men and friends around him. He is wealthy and has vehicles. He is religious and pays homage to gods, Brahmins and religious preceptors.

CONJUNCTIONS OF JUPITER

Jupiter and Venus

When Jupiter and Venus are together, the native is religious, intelligent, learned and rich. He may earn by virtue of his scholarship. He is endowed with many meritorious qualities. His marriage partner comes from a high family or is a noble person and he will have conjugal happiness in full measure. He will be chivalrous and a favorite of the king.

When the two planets are in the Ascendant, the native has a forgiving disposition. He abides by the advice of his religious preceptors and seniors. He attains a high position in life.

If the conjunction takes place in the Fourth, the native vanquishes his enemies. He has good friends, relations and vehicles. He pays homage to gods, Brahmins and religious preceptors.

If the two planets are in the Seventh, he has a good marriage and is wealthy. He attains a good name and fame and leads a comfortable life, but has more daughters than sons. He has excellent vehicles.

The effects described for the Tenth house are very good. The native possesses many luxury items or consumer goods and commands immense respect. He has a very agreeable temper. He is wealthy, has a number of servants and occupies a kingly position.

According to the *Horasara*, if the two planets are in the First, Fifth, Eighth or Ninth the native will have a good spouse and children and will be wealthy, but if they are in any house other than those listed above he will be troubled by some chronic disease. The *Horasara* is an ancient text written by Prithuyashas, who was the son of Varaha Mihira, but in our view Prithuyashas has been influenced more by the fact that Jupiter and Venus are enemies[6] rather than by their inherent benefic qualities. We feel that Jupiter and Venus in conjunction will show their best effects for people born with a Gemini Ascendant.

Jupiter and Saturn

If Jupiter and Saturn are together, the native is very chivalrous and wealthy. He may be the mayor of a town or the president of an assembly (in a modern context we might say that he may be chairman of a commission, the head of a union or some similar position). He attains name and fame. According to the *Jataka Parijata*, he may be a good craftsman. Varaha Mihira states that the native can excel as a barber or as a manufacturer of utensils. He may deal in grain or food products. Such a person is generous. One view is that Jupiter stands for good and open

---

6   In classical Hindu astrology, planets are either friendly or inimical to each other depending on the elements of the signs they rule. Hence a planet that rules fire and water signs, like Jupiter, is an enemy of Venus, which rules earth and air signs.

actions, while Saturn acts in a low and hidden manner. Their conjunction would lead to actions wherein the features of both planets are present. There is an astrological aphorism that Jupiter indicates wealth and prosperity while Saturn stands for adversity. When the two combine, mixed effects are felt.

When Jupiter and Saturn conjoin in the First, the native is indolent and cruel. He is learned and wealthy, but will have only a fraction of happiness (i.e. he is not fully happy). He is wicked. We feel that if Sagittarius or Pisces is rising, the conjunction of the above planets in the Ascendant will show very good effects.

If the two planets are in the Fourth, the native will have good friends and relations. He will be on affectionate terms with others. He will have good health and become a minister. He will be victorious in a contest, strife or warfare.

If the two planets conjoin in the Seventh, the native will be chivalrous but addicted to some kind of vice. He will be wicked and unattractive. He will be dull-witted and avaricious of his father's wealth. He will lose his wealth on account of enmity with a woman or with women generally.

If the two planets combine in the Tenth, the native owns many cattle and conveyances. He has only a few sons. He is a favorite of the king and occupies a high position.

According to the *Horasara*, if the conjunction takes place in the First, Second, Fourth, Fifth, Seventh, Eighth, Ninth or Twelfth house the native will be devoid of wealth and respect. But if the two planets are in the Third, Sixth, Tenth or Eleventh house the native becomes famous and is respected by the king.

VENUS AND SATURN

When Venus and Saturn conjoin, the native is efficient in calligraphy, painting, etc. His wealth increases due to patronage extended by the opposite sex. According to the *Jataka Parijata,* the native will be an athlete and own cattle. He is fond of traveling and is clever in timber work and artisanship. He may also be a good surgeon.

If Venus and Saturn are in the Ascendant, the native has an amiable personality and many sexual liaisons. He is rich and leads a comfortable life. He has a number of servants but suffers sorrows.

When the two planets are in the Fourth, the native gains money from his friends and is respected by his relations. He also receives honors and riches from the government.

When the conjunction takes place in the Seventh, the native gains money from his friends and is respected by his relations. He also receives honors and riches from the government.

When the conjunction of Venus and Saturn takes place in the Seventh, the native enjoys sexual pleasures. He is very wealthy and has a happy life with the damsels. He earns a good reputation.

If the planets conjoin in the Tenth, the native may become a minister or king. He performs noble deeds, becomes famous, and is free from all mental perplexities.

In our view the conjunction will show its best effects if the two planets are in Libra, or when either Taurus, Libra, Capricorn or Aquarius is the Ascendant. According to the *Horasara*, if the conjunction takes place in the First, Fourth, Fifth, Ninth or Tenth house the native will be under the influence of his spouse (or the opposite sex), will be wealthy, and will occupy a high rank under the king. But if the conjunction takes place in a house other than those mentioned above, the native is devoid of wealth and stamina.[7]

---

7 See also Chapter 7 for specific effects in the Ninth house.

2
CONJUNCTIONS
OF THREE PLANETS

The general principle is that if malefics combine it is evil; on the other hand, the conjunction of benefics is good. Varaha Mihira, in Chapter 14 of his *Hora Shastra,* first delineates the effects of two planets and then states that when more than two planets combine the effects of the three pairs of planets as described above should be blended to arrive at the resultant effect of the combination of the three planets. For example, the effect of the Sun and the Moon together has been delineated; so also of a Moon-Mars or Sun-Mars conjunction. All these effects must be blended to arrive at the effect of the Sun, Moon and Mars conjoining in one house.

It is necessary to point out that the effects described above of the blending of two or more planets is based on their natural or inherent qualities. But the sign they occupy will also be an important factor. For example, Saturn in the First house makes one uncouth and of low mentality, but Saturn in Libra in the Ascendant has often been treated as a veritable rajayoga. Or to take another example: Saturn in Sagittarius or Pisces in the Ascendant has been praised by astrologers, and Saturn and Jupiter together in the First house will be a very good combination if the rising sign is Sagittarius or Pisces.

To cite yet another example, Venus in Scorpio is not good. The Moon in that sign is debilitated, so how can the Moon and Venus in Scorpio show the same effects as the Moon and Venus in Taurus, where the Moon would be exalted and Venus in its own sign? These different shadings, attributable to the sign position, must always be kept in mind. Otherwise one's judgment is likely to be faulty. Another factor which greatly influences the resultant effect is the house position. Some older authors have also described the influence generated by their location in angles. The *Horasara* often adds the provision that the effect is such and such in a particular set of houses, while in other houses the effects will be otherwise. No old master has delineated the effects of conjunctions in *each* of the twelve houses. An encyclopedic compilation of the effects of conjunctions in each house and sign would be a valuable reference book. But unfortunately no such work exists.

The influence will also vary according to the lordship of the house or houses in question. For example, when Aries is rising, a combination of the Sun and Mars would be a conjunction of the lord of the First (an angle) and the Fifth (a trine), and as such would be very good. But if Gemini is rising, the same conjunction would be a combination of the lords of the Third, Sixth and Eleventh — an evil combination. Or to take another example, if Gemini is rising a combination of Jupiter and Venus would be very good, particularly in Pisces in the Tenth house, for it would be a conjunction of the lords of a trine (the Fifth) and two angles (the Seventh and Tenth), but if Sagittarius is rising it will be a combination of the lords of the First, Fourth, Sixth and Eleventh, which is not so good because the lord of the Sixth pulls the others down. Thus there are innumerable permutations and combinations and no work, howsoever exhaustive, could delineate every possible effect.

Allied to the subject matter under discussion is another point, and that is the influence produced by the lord of a house occupying a particular house. This not only applies to cases where there is a conjunction, but also when there is no conjunction. The lord of the First house may occupy any one of the twelve houses, thus producing twelve possible shades of nuance. The effect of the lord of the Second house will likewise vary depending on which of the twelve houses it occupies.

Thus it will be seen that the ingredients for judging a conjunction or aspect of two or more planets are:

1. The inherent attributes of the planets
2. Their ownership of particular houses
3. The house position of any given house lord
4. The sign occupied by the planets, and
5. The aspects they receive from other planets.

We shall have occasion to observe that aspects greatly modify the influence of any combination. We deal with the modifying influences of aspects in Chapters 4 through 6 and shall not enlarge upon the subject here. A comprehensive set of guidelines is detailed in the last chapter.

CONJUNCTIONS OF THE SUN

Sun, Moon and Mars

The native will be skilled in mechanics or the manufacture of machinery and clever in various undertakings; he crushes his opponents, but is shameless and given to evil deeds. He is wealthy and politic. The native has some infirmity in one of his limbs, does not enjoy happiness in respect to his marriage and children, and may not live long. (One must, however, look to various other indications when deciding upon one's longevity).

Sun, Moon and Mercury

The native is persevering and engages in government service; he is very intelligent, assertive and forceful, wise and clever, has academic and literary tastes, and is fond of company and drinks. He rises to a high position due to his literary merits.

Sun, Moon and Jupiter

The native has a fiery temper and is clever in hypocrisy; he is efficient as a servant and fond of traveling abroad. He is very intelligent with a good memory but a changeable disposition. He is learned and a favorite of the king.

Sun, Moon and Venus

The native is attached to another's spouse, cruel, learned, wealthy, and afraid of his enemies. He is cunning in appropriating other people's wealth and spouses.

Sun, Moon and Saturn

The native is not wealthy and suffers from some chronic disease, is miserable and infirm in one of his limbs. He is intent upon seeking favors from others; he earns his livelihood by serving others. The native is not intelligent but contentious, having an unsatisfied lust; he likes to travel abroad, is deceptive and wicked.

Sun, Mars and Mercury

The native will be opposed to religious rites or act in ways contrary to righteous conduct. He is miserly and merciless but courageous; he will suffer due to destruction of his earned wealth. He is shameless but may excel in wrestling. He does not have happiness in respect to his spouse or children. But if these planets combine in a good house the native may have a good marriage and children.

Sun, Mars and Jupiter

The native is learned and very wealthy, respected by people, healthy, devoid of enemies, and leads an all-around comfortable life. He has a forceful personality and is at times aggressive; he is also very clever in speech and may occupy a very high position. He will do good to others and will be popular.

Sun, Mars and Venus

The native is good looking but will suffer from some eye disease; he will be born in a good family (or his conduct will be gentlemanly) and he will enjoy luxuries and be wealthy. But at times, he will use piercing language which will hurt others.

Sun, Mars and Saturn

The native is not intelligent; he will suffer from infirmity in one of his limbs and be devoid of wealth. He will have some chronic disease. His conduct will be sinful and he will deceive others' spouses; he may suffer from fire, poison or confinement, and he will die abroad in a place other than his homeland.

Sun, Mercury and Jupiter

The native is learned, wise and intelligent, a favorite of the king; he will enjoy luxury at other peoples' expense. He will cause harm to others and will be wealthy but become poor in old age. He may suffer from eye disease. The native will also be clever in and fond of arts and crafts.

Sun, Mercury and Venus

The native will have a soft body and a luxurious and splendid living; he will be learned, courageous, and will command respect. He will be happy in respect to parents and relations if the Fourth and Tenth houses are well fortified, otherwise he lives separately from them. The native is very talkative and fond of traveling. He suffers in respect to marital happiness.

Sun, Mercury and Saturn

The native suffers from bilious diseases and also due to corruption of blood, has a weak constitution, and his veins are prominent in his body. He is antagonistic to his own people, lives abroad, and is not prosperous. He will be wicked and envious. His mannerisms will be similar to those of an important man.

Sun, Jupiter and Venus

The native is intelligent, generous in giving, very famous, and occupies a high position, but he loses his wealth due to the opposite sex and gambling, and is troubled by enemies. The combination is good for happiness in respect to spouse and children; the native obliges others by rendering service to them.

Sun, Jupiter and Saturn

The native does not have a well proportioned body but he is fearless, respected, and a favorite of the king. He has benevolent inclinations but is antagonistic to his relations; he has a good spouse, children and friends.

Sun, Venus and Saturn

The native is always agitated due to fear from enemies, does not command respect, is vain, and does not have academic or literary tastes. His conduct is not good and he may suffer from leprosy (in countries where leprosy has been eradicated, this old axiom might nevertheless indicate the presence of serious skin disease). The native is deceitful and miserable and does not earn well in life; in old age his finances may improve.

CONJUNCTIONS OF THE MOON

Moon, Mars and Mercury

The native will be famous, respected by people, and eloquent, but poor during the middle portion of life. But according to the *Jataka Parijata*, the native is a glutton; he does not do good deeds and sullies others. Kalyan Varma states that the native is devoid of good relations; his conduct is sinful.

Moon, Mars and Jupiter

The native's body has scars from wounds, but an attractive appearance nevertheless. The native is love-sick; he is a favorite of ladies whom he covets greatly, but he is also fierce in anger. If the combination occurs in Scorpio, Cancer or Capricorn or in the Sixth, Seventh, Eighth or Twelfth house, the native is not wealthy; but if the conjunction is in some other sign or house, the native will be wealthy and powerful.

Moon, Mars and Venus

The native has impudent sons; he is fond of traveling. Neither the native's mother nor his wife is of good temper. He is allergic to cold.

Moon, Mars and Saturn

The native's mother may die at an early age or there may be a premature separation from her. The native does not get on well with people; he is mean-minded, unpopular and wicked. He is also fickle minded. If the combination takes place in the Ascendant, Ninth or Tenth house, he lives in a place other than his homeland; he does not have the company of his relations, but leads a comfortable life anyway.

Moon, Mercury and Jupiter

The native is healthy, learned, eloquent, lustrous, wealthy, renowned and very popular; he has many brothers and sons. He is a favorite of the king (i.e. occupies a high position).

Moon, Mercury and Venus

The native, though learned, will be envious of others. He will be avaricious and his actions will not be good.

Moon, Mercury and Saturn

The native is eloquent. He has an inclination to sacrifice his wealth for a good cause. He is respected by the king and occupies a high position. He has many merits, but does not enjoy good health; he suffers from an infirmity in some limb.

Moon, Jupiter and Venus

The native is the son of a good lady; he is learned and intelligent, proficient, of a good appearance, kind and gentle. He will have good children, a number of vehicles, a host of followers, and he will be very wealthy.

Moon, Jupiter and Saturn

The native becomes the head of a village, town or institution. He is very learned, fond of women, and he has the company of an older woman (or he may have a liaison with a woman older than himself). He will be a friend of people who speak sweetly, devoted to the gods, his parents and religious preceptors. He will have good children.

Moon, Venus and Saturn

The native may excel in the study of scriptures, calligraphy, painting or astrology, and he may act as a religious priest. He will be of pleasing appearance and be popular. He will be rich and kind-hearted. He leads a comfortable life and occupies a fairly good position.

CONJUNCTIONS OF MARS

Mars, Mercury and Jupiter

The native is inclined to help others. He has literary or poetic tastes, is a connoisseur of music, drama and dancing, has a good wife, and occupies a good position.

Mars, Mercury and Venus

The native does not belong to a good family, suffers from infirmity in some limb, is fickle-minded and wicked, very optimistic and garrulous. According to the *Horasara*, the native is slightly sickly during childhood, is well mannered and well versed in arts and poetry, and occupies a good position.

Mars, Mercury and Saturn

The native has dark eyes, follows a career in the services, lives abroad (at a place other than his homeland), has some disease in the mouth or eyes (or face), and has the company of humorous people. According to the *Jataka Parijata*, the native has eye diseases, wanders or travels much, and runs errands for others. According to the *Horasara*, the native's wife may be of loose morals or he himself may have a liaison with a woman of loose morals. He antagonizes his relations, is poor and short-lived. His cattle perish. His wife may also have a premature end.

Mars, Jupiter and Venus

The native is a favorite of the king, has good children, has enjoyment in the company of damsels, and leads a comfortable and luxurious life. He will own properties and vehicles and will be renowned. He will please everyone.

Mars, Jupiter and Saturn

The native has some marks or wounds on the body; he is without compassion, and not of good conduct. Condemned by his friends, he is nevertheless a favorite of the king. The native has a weak constitution and does not enjoy good health. He is proud. According to the *Horasara*, the native is courageous and capable of putting up with a great deal of hardship. He is envious, but wealthy and strong. He occupies a good position.

Mars, Venus and Saturn

The native is devoid of happiness, and always lives at a place other than his homeland. He does not have good sons. He suffers humiliation or punishment at the hands of the government. His mother may not be of good conduct or he may be prematurely separated from her. His spouse may not be of good conduct either or he himself may be attached to a person with loose morals. He does not behave like a gentleman.

CONJUNCTIONS OF MERCURY

Mecury, Jupiter and Venus

This is a splendid combination and will enhance the good effects of the house tenanted. In general, the native has a handsome body; he is very rich, occupies a kingly position, is healthy and renowned. He is truthful in speech and conduct. He vanquishes his enemies and is powerful.

Mercury, Jupiter and Saturn

The native is intelligent and wealthy and has many luxuries; he leads a comfortable life, is attached to his wife, has perseverance and happiness. He has a good personality.

Mercury, Venus and Saturn

The native is wealthy but cunning, untruthful in speech but very garrulous, not even-tempered, but clever in arts and sciences. He is fond of his homeland and may live there. He has a liaison with another's spouse, is of firm determination and long lived, and becomes famous and popular.

JUPITER, VENUS AND SATURN

Though born in a humble family, the native rises to a very high position and becomes renowned. He is courteous and well-mannered and leads a happy life. He has family happiness. His gains will be sufficient to keep him comfortable and his enjoyments are not excessive. He is popular.

✳ ✳ ✳

This brings to an end the delineation of the effects arising from three planets in conjunction. Because of the reasons stated earlier, it would be too much to expect the descriptions to fit each individual chart like a glove. However, the general principle will be found to hold good that the combination of benefics is good and that of malefics is evil. Another point mentioned in the *Jataka Parijata* must also be given due weight. This ancient Sanskrit text states that if benefics conjoin the Moon, it is good in respect to happiness pertaining to the mother. If, on the other hand, the Moon is in conjunction with malefics, it portends ill for the mother. This is so because in all nativities the Moon is the significator of the mother. By the same token, because the Sun is the significator for the father it is good for the native in respect to his father when the Sun is in the company of benefics, and ill if this luminary is conjoined with malefics.

The Sun and Moon are the two most important planets. The Sun stands for the soul and the Moon for the heart and emotions. If these two are strong, the native can overcome all impediments and cut a way for himself through life. But if they are weak, the native is not even able to take full advantage of other good planets.

In this connection we must not forget that even though the *general* significance of the planets is the same in all charts, the *particular* significance will change according to the ownership of houses. For example, if the lord of the First house is in evil company and the lord of the Seventh in good association, the native may be sickly or lack an assertive personality but may have a very good spouse. This is on the principle that the lord of the First is afflicted while the lord of the Seventh is well placed. This principle must be applied to the lords of all the houses.

The idea behind studying these delineations is to cultivate the faculty of astrological discrimination and appraisal. In culling out these delineations from the ancient Sanskrit texts we have tried to be as faithful to the old masters as possible. But due allowance has to be made for the ancient terminology. "A kingly position" must be interpreted in the modern context as a successful or high-status position, and not as a position equal to that of a modern king. When these texts were written in India, there were tens of thousands of kings in the land. With these comments we pass on to the conjunction of four or more planets.

3
MULTIPLE
CONJUNCTIONS

CONJUNCTIONS OF FOUR PLANETS

THE SUN

Sun, Moon, Mars and Mercury
Writer, copyist or painter, good in calligraphy, talkative, but not of good health; clever and cunning to the point of employing stratagems and artifices.

Sun, Moon, Mars and Jupiter
Rich, respected by the opposite sex; diplomatic, asertive and vigorous; does not harbor sorrow (i.e. is not pessimistic); given to action; capable and clever in achieving his aims.

Sun, Moon, Mars and Venus
Speech and conduct are gentlemanly; comfortable life; clever; given to accumulating wealth; well educated, having happiness in respect to wife and sons.

Sun, Moon, Mars and Saturn
Parts of the body are not proportionate, or there is an infirmity in some limb; not tall, devoid of wealth, solicits others' help for living; mixes with all kinds of people; not intelligent or wise.

Sun, Moon, Mercury and Jupiter
Deals in gold (or other Jupiterian commodities); prominent eyes; an artisan or connoisseur of the arts; persevering; very rich, with an attractive body.

Sun, Moon, Mercury and Venus
Agitated; of comely appearance; eloquent; not a large body; a favorite of the king (i.e. of the government).

Sun, Moon, Mercury and Saturn

Separated from parent(s) due to death or other circumstances; devoid of wealth and happiness; not truthful; given to traveling; solicits favors for his living.

Sun, Moon, Jupiter and Venus

Lord of water (reservoirs, ponds, lakes) and forests; owns cattle; a happy and comfortable living; clever; respected and honored by the king (i.e. by the government).

Sun, Moon, Jupiter and Saturn

Aggressive and sharp-tempered; several sons and much wealth; adored by good (i.e. beautiful) damsels or has a beautiful wife of a good family.

Sun, Moon, Venus and Saturn

Behaves like a female; always forward, having a lean and thin body (i.e. constitutionally not robust or troubled by a chronic disease); not bold; diffident at all times.

Sun, Mars, Mercury and Jupiter

Brave and valorous; engaged in productive activity; following an occupation connected with rotating machines; suffers in respect to wife and health; given to traveling; not happy.

Sun, Mars, Mercury and Venus

Does not have proportionate limbs (i.e. there is a disease in some part of the body); not much stamina; wicked intentions; thievish tendencies; liaison with another's spouse.

Sun, Mars, Mercury and Saturn

A fighter (literally or figuratively); intelligent and wise but sharp-tempered; low conduct; excellence in writing, expression or poetry; rises to a high position (analogous to that of a minister or a king).

Sun, Mars, Jupiter and Venus

Comely appearance; much respected by the people; wealthy; wins the approbation or favors of the king (i.e. government); renowned and very diplomatic.

Sun, Mars, Jupiter and Saturn

Proud, respected by the clans (i.e. groups of people or associations); accomplishes his objectives; endearing to friends and relations; is a favorite of the king (i.e. government).

Sun, Mars, Venus and Saturn

Restless, agitated (or having a chronic ailment in some part of the body); of low conduct; having an oblique glance (or both eyes are unequal); inimical to relations, suffers defeat or humiliation.

Sun, Mercury, Jupiter and Venus

Wealthy; leads a happy and comfortable life; successful in endeavors and with relations; attains a high position.

Sun, Mercury, Jupiter and Saturn

Behaves like a eunuch; proud; fond of quarreling; has siblings from the same mother but has little enthusiasm.

Sun, Mercury, Venus and Saturn

Has a handsome appearance; intelligent; eloquent; comfortable life; purity in conduct; has good stamina; patient and persevering; helpful to friends (or benefits from the cooperation of friends).

Sun, Jupiter, Venus and Saturn

Avaricious; skilled in composition (prose or poetry); occupies a prominent position; commands artisans and workmen; controls or leads low people; becomes a favorite of the king (i.e. government).

THE MOON

Moon, Mars, Mercury and Jupiter

Knowledgeable in the shastras (i.e. learned treatises); highly intelligent; attains a high position such as that of a king or minister.

Moon, Mars, Mercury and Venus

Good to look at but fond of quarreling; inclined to much sleeping (or frequently dozing); of low conduct; has a liaison with a profligate; inimical to relations; not happy.

Moon, Mars, Mercury and Saturn

Chivalrous; premature separation from parents; does not belong to a good family; has several wives and many friends; engages in good deeds.

Moon, Mars, Jupiter and Venus

Has an infirmity in some limb; has a good spouse and much forbearance; receives much respect (or is very proud); intelligent; has many comforts and friends.

Moon, Mars, Jupiter and Saturn

Deaf or hard of hearing (this infirmity may develop later in life); wealthy; chivalrous; insane (i.e. may develop schizophrenia or some other mental aberration); clever in speech; of stable temperament; intelligent and generous.

Moon, Mars, Venus and Saturn

Bold and intrepid; always excited or agitated; has a liaison with an adulterous person; has eyes like those of a snake.

Moon, Mercury, Jupiter and Venus

Learned; prematurely separated from parents; has a handsome appearance or is very attractive; wealthy; has no enemies or overcomes them.

Moon, Mercury, Jupiter and Saturn

Very religious; has much fame; foremost; intelligent, brilliant, fond of relations (or adored by relations); noted for his excellent compositions (prose or poetry); becomes a minister to a king.

Moon, Mercury, Venus and Saturn

Inclined to have a liaison with another's spouse; his own spouse is ungentle and troublesome; has no relations or is not affected by them; learned but inimical to other people and unpopular.

Moon, Jupiter, Venus and Saturn

Of handsome appearance; distressed; fond of traveling; suffers from skin diseases; talks much but is of truthful conduct; devoid of mother (early separation from her).

MARS

Mars, Mercury, Jupiter and Venus

Chivalrous, intelligent, learned; eloquent but devoid of wealth; pure and truthful in conduct; disputatious; capable of putting up with confrontations.

Mars, Mercury, Jupiter and Saturn

A fighter, brought up or supported by others; hard and muscular; very intent upon duels or conflicts; famous; fond of keeping dogs.

Mars, Jupiter, Venus and Saturn

Brilliant; wealthy; easily tempted by women (i.e. of a very flirtatious disposition); courageous and easily engaged in daring ventures; very nimble; cunning to the point of lying and cheating.

MERCURY

Mercury, Jupiter, Venus and Saturn

Given to studies; has a very good memory (and is therefore learned); infatuated with women; proves very reliable in employment.

✳ ✳ ✳

The above gives an idea of the lines along which the ancients summed up the effect of conjunctions of four planets. Historical conditions have changed though basic planetary characteristics have not. Therefore we have occasionally substituted the word "government" for "king" and so on. In ancient polities, kingship equaled government and vice-versa. In classical India, there were thousands of political territories, hence thousands of kings and many thousands of ministers. In a modern context, these terms should not be taken literally, but should be reasonably interpreted.

Astrologers must also exercise judgment in interpreting words and phrases such as "talkative" or "not of good health" applied to the Sun-Moon-Mars-Mercury combination. If Mercury is strong one's speech will be learned and logical, but if Mercury is weak the native will be shallow and garrulous. The Moon weak in digital strength (i.e. before the eighth day of its waxing cycle or after the eighth day of its waning cycle) may make one unhealthy — particularly women. So also the Sun and Mars together may give excessive heat (i.e. excess Pitta, see footnote, Chapter 1, p. 17). Or take the description of Sun-Mars-Mercury-Venus. The expression "thievish tendencies" may, on the lowest level, indicate only petty larceny, while on a higher plane it may signify tax evasion involving millions. Sun-Jupiter-Venus-Saturn "commands artisans and workmen." In a modern context this may mean that one works as a manager or trade union leader. The effect of Moon-Mars-Mercury-Saturn speaks of "several wives." In many countries polygamy is illegal (in India it is thus for

Hindus). So this phrase no longer signifies the marrying of several women, but merely the enjoyment of them. The interpretation is, therefore, left to the judicious understanding of the reader.

These guidelines are not only for conjunctions of four planets but for two, three, five or more planets. The above effects for conjunctions of four planets have been described in the context of a householder's life. But some astrological aphorisms also state that a conjunction of four or more planets may lead the native to relinquish the householder's life, renounce the world, and turn into an ascetic. This point will be dealt with at the end of this chapter.

CONJUNCTIONS OF FIVE PLANETS

THE SUN

Sun, Moon, Mars, Mercury and Jupiter

Sorrowful; distressed due to separation from spouse; given to much display and manifestation (i.e. illusion as distinct from reality).

Sun, Moon, Mars, Mercury and Venus

Always engaged in other people's work; loses vitality and stamina due to friends and relations; has the friendship and company of impotent persons.

Sun, Moon, Mars, Mercury and Saturn

May not be long-lived; humble; devoid of comforts and happiness; without a spouse, son or wealth; liable to confinement.

Sun, Moon, Mars, Jupiter and Venus

May be blind or suffering from some vision problem; much distressed; abandoned (or uncared for) by parents; fond of music and singing.

Sun, Moon, Mars, Jupiter and Saturn

Clever in warfare (i.e. a strategist in life's struggles); very capable; appropriates others' wealth and causes distress to others; has a mercurial sense of activity but can be a back-biter.

Sun, Moon, Mars, Venus and Saturn

Devoid of rest, wealth or luxuries; of low conduct; has liaisons with others' wives.

Sun, Moon, Mercury, Jupiter and Venus
Skilled in mechanics; very wealthy; may become a minister or holds a magisterial office; renowned and of good reputation.

Sun, Moon, Mercury, Jupiter and Saturn
Wanting in courage and bereft of well-wishers; may become insane; hypocritical and a bully, but dependent on others.

Sun, Moon, Mercury, Venus and Saturn
Tall, hairy body and enthusiastic throughout life; devoid of happiness, wealth and son.

Sun, Moon, Mercury, Venus and Saturn
Eloquent, skilled in mysticism or jugglery; fickle (in resolutions or emotions); a beloved of damsels; has many enemies but is fearless.

Sun, Moon, Jupiter, Venus and Saturn
Generous, philanthropic, and possessed of a good income; practical; a favorite of the king (i.e. of the government); may become a recluse in old age.

Sun, Mars, Mercury, Jupiter and Venus
Handsome appearance; highly sexed; has many horses and many good deeds to his credit; commands an army; has no sorrows or anxieties (i.e. is optimistic); a favorite of the king (i.e. government).

Sun, Mars, Mercury, Jupiter and Saturn
Oppressed by ailments and enemies; may be evicted from his place (office or residence); much distressed by sorrows; wanders about dejected and depressed.

Sun, Mars, Jupiter, Venus and Saturn
Skilled in mechanics or in projects connected with water, metallurgy and chemicals; attains name and fame due to his excellence in these subjects.

Sun, Mercury, Jupiter, Venus and Saturn
A great scholar and well versed in the interpretation of books of learning; does good to friends (or himself benefits from friends); a favorite of his teachers and preceptors; very religious and compassionate.

THE MOON

Moon, Mars, Mercury, Jupiter and Venus

A gentleman; healthy; endowed with learning, wealth and happiness; truthful; does good to his relations (or is very friendly with his relations); has many friends.

Moon, Mars, Mercury, Jupiter and Saturn

Suffers from night blindness; poor and humble; dependent upon others for his livelihood; brings shame to his family.

Moon, Mars, Mercury, Venus and Saturn

Suffers from physical assaults or illness; likely to be confined or imprisoned; poor and agitated; learned and respected, though not very even-tempered; has many friends and many enemies.

Moon, Mars, Jupiter, Venus and Saturn

Runs errands for others; not very learned; does not have much virility; unfortunate; devoid of wealth; agitated (mentally anxious or suffering from some physical ailment).

Moon, Mercury, Jupiter, Venus and Saturn

A minister or one equal to a king; head of a clan or of groups of people and societies; is held in high esteem.

MARS

Mars With Four Other Planets

Wise and resolute but mentally unstable; does not harbor sorrow (i.e. is optimistic); feels sleepy at odd hours; not wealthy; a great favorite of the king.

CONJUNCTIONS OF SIX PLANETS

Sun, Moon, Mars, Mercury, Jupiter and Venus

Lean and thin body; highly intelligent and wise; wealthy; devoted to studies and religion.

Sun, Moon, Mars, Mercury, Jupiter and Saturn

Generous to others; has many sterling qualities; is engaged in other people's work but fickle-minded; inclined to live in a solitary place.

Sun, Moon, Mars, Mercury, Venus and Saturn

Inclined to theft or appropriating others' property; has liaisons with others' wives; not respected by his people; not wise; devoid of happiness in respect to a son.

Sun, Moon, Mars, Jupiter, Venus and Saturn

Low in position, in conduct, or in both; works for others and suffers from a wasting disease (breathing trouble or asthma); not well spoken of by his relatives.

Sun, Moon, Mercury, Jupiter, Venus and Saturn

Attains a high position such as that of a minister; enjoys prosperity; has a forbearing and forgiving temperament; sorrowful and devoid of wealth; suffers in respect to matrimonial happiness.

Sun, Mars, Mercury, Jupiter, Venus and Saturn

Lives in forests or on mountains; visits holy places of pilgrimage; devoid of wealth; no happiness in respect to a son.

Moon, Mars, Mercury, Jupiter, Venus and Saturn

Clean in body and dress; illustrious but attached to many young damsels; rises to the position of minister; a favorite of the king (government); wealthy and prosperous; happiness in respect to sons.

CONJUNCTION OF ALL SEVEN PLANETS

A wanderer; not very neat in appearance; devoid of wealth and learning; an inferior artisan; physically indolent or mentally slow to grasp things.

HARMONY AND HETEROGENEITY

The ancients have not rated the combination of four or more planets as very positive, and an eminent classical author states that such a combination generally leads to the impairment of wealth, wisdom and happiness; but a perusal of the preceding few pages will show that this is not always so. The principle that a combination of four or more planets weakens the good effects of individual planets emanates from the idea that when there are four or more units there is bound to be a combination of some harmonious and some heterogeneous influences.

What do we mean by harmony and heterogeneity? In the context of planets, these are polarities which arise due to two factors: first, the natural characteristics of a planet as inherently benefic or malefic, and second, the lordship. In discussing the conjunctions or aspects of planets, the classical texts have taken into consideration the first factor only, and we shall also confine ourselves to it here. (We shall discuss lordship at a subsequent stage.) Harmony is when a natural benefic is conjoined with another natural benefic. There is disharmony when a natural benefic and a natural malefic combine. And when a natural malefic conjoins with another natural malefic there is heterogeneity.

In Hindu astrology the word used for a natural benefic is *shubha*, and for a natural malefic *papa*. *Shubha* literally means "auspicious" and *papa* means "sinful." The general rule is that the Moon, Mercury, Jupiter and Venus are deemed benefic, while the Sun, Mars and Saturn are treated as malefic. The classical authorities, however, note some exceptions to the rule. They say that a waxing Moon is *shubha*, while a waning Moon is not. Others state that when the Moon is applying to the Sun and from the time it is within 24° of the Sun until conjunction (i.e. new Moon), it is a malefic; otherwise it is a benefic.

In the case of Mercury, which is quick to absorb the qualities of the planet with which it is conjoined, it is often deemed a benefic when conjunct a benefic and malefic if conjoined with a malefic. Varaha Mihira, an ancient Hindu astrologer, supports this view in Chapter 2, verse 5 of his *Brihat Jataka*, but in Chapter 1, verse 19, he states that a sign aspected or tenanted by its lord, Jupiter, and/or Mercury becomes strong provided it is not tenanted or aspected by any other planets. The same principle has been reiterated in Varaha Mihira's other work, *Laghu Jataka* (Chapter 1, verse 14). We agree that the beneficence of a planet is always *impaired* by conjunction with a malefic (and particularly so in the case of Mercury, which, being mercurial, is quick in the transmission of both objective and subjective efforts), but we also support Varaha Mihira's view that Mercury should always be treated as a natural benefic. In calculating the strength of a house, Mercury's aspect is, again, always treated as benefic. (See more references to Mercury in the discussion below.)

Venus is also deemed a benefic, though Rudra Bhatta in his *Vivarana* (a Sanskrit text, c. 1,000 AD) states on page 34 that the aspect of Venus is not good. But the subtlety implied in the *occupancy* of Venus being a good influence upon a house while its *aspect* is not good is generally not observed. In the *Hora Shastra*, Chapter 13, verse 1, Varaha Mihira states that if the Moon is in its own navamsha[1] or in his great friend's navamsha, and if such a Moon is aspected by Jupiter in a diurnal chart or by Venus in a nocturnal chart, the native is wealthy and leads a happy and comfortable life. According to the *Brihat Jataka,* Chapter 13, verse 2, the *Jataka Parijata,* Chapter 1, verses 113 and 114, and the *Phala Deepika,* Chapter 6, verse 42, if Mercury, Jupiter and Venus are in the Sixth, Seventh or Eighth houses from the Moon or the Ascendant (in any order — all in one, two or three houses), extremely good results flow from such a combination. Also, if Mercury, Jupiter and Venus are in the Third, Sixth, Tenth or Eleventh (in any order, in any one or more of the above houses), the native becomes very wealthy (see *Brihat Jataka,* Chapter 13, verse 9, and *Phala Deepika*, Chapter 6, verse 19). So in practice Venus is treated as a benefic. Thus the Moon (only when applying to the Sun and within 24°), the Sun, Mars and Saturn in ascending order are increasingly malefic. According to Rudra Bhatta the Sun, if in his own sign or exaltation (i.e. Leo or Aries), is not *papa* but only *krura* (cruel).

All this discussion about *shubha* and *papa* should be understood in the context of harmonious and heterogeneous combinations. When several planets (five or more) combine, there is bound to be a heterogeneous configuration, some planets being *shubhas* and others *papas*. Thus Kalyan Varma, another classical writer, states: "Generally, when five or six planets are together the native is unhappy; devoid of wealth, intelligence and wisdom." Why generally? Because, as readers will have observed in the preceding pages, there are a few combinations of five or six planets which have been described as good and promising.

CONJUNCTIONS LEADING TO ASCETICISM

According to standard texts, the conjunctions discussed in this section lead to asceticism. But before we enumerate them, it would be relevant to note that in ancient India taking up *sanyasa* (withdrawing oneself from all worldly preoccupations) was considered one of the ultimate goals of Hindu philosophy and the Hindu way of life. Hence a large number of

---

1   The term navamsha defines a special chart or varga (literally "division") derived by dividing each sign of the zodiac into nine parts, each part ruled by a particular planet. The sign occupied by a planet in the navamsha chart is considered almost as important as its position in the basic natal horoscope.

people took to asceticism, particularly in the last quarter of life. There were different kinds of asceticism, as well as established canons for entry into certain ascetic orders. For example, only a *Brahmin* could become a *dandi sanyasi. Dandi* means "one who carries a stick as an emblem of a particular order." *Sanyasi* means an ascetic. The classical authors have broadly divided the ascetic orders into seven categories and have stated that one takes to a particular order depending upon which of the seven planets is strongest:

The Sun	Muni
The Moon	Any of the Shaivite or Vaishnavite orders
Mars	Shakya (a Buddhist order)
Mercury	Ajiwaka
Jupiter	Bhikshu (an order both Hindu and Buddhist)
Venus	Charaka (practicing yoga and clever in medicine but likely to be hypocritical)
Saturn	Nirgranthi (leading a nomadic life, observing no code, perhaps wandering naked)

We will not go into detail about these orders, first because they have become obsolete even in India, and second because they are only of interest to Hindus. There are ascetics all over the world, Buddhists, Christians, Muslims, Zoroastrians, etc., some following the strict and narrow paths prescribed by their respective religions, others loosely wedded to their faith and holding to the form but not to the spirit. This applies to Hindus also. There are more charlatans than real ascetics. One frequently comes across people clad in saffron robes, but only a microscopic minority is immune to the desires of the flesh or from the vices common to householders.

Now we will give the combinations of planets leading to asceticism.

Four Planets

1. Sun, Moon, Mars and Mercury
2. Sun, Moon, Mars and Venus
3. Sun, Moon, Mars and Saturn
4. Sun, Moon, Mercury and Venus
5. Sun, Moon, Mercury and Saturn
6. Sun, Moon, Jupiter and Saturn
7. Sun, Moon, Venus and Saturn
8. Sun, Mars, Mercury and Jupiter
9. Sun, Mars, Mercury and Venus
10. Sun, Mars, Mercury and Saturn

11. Sun, Mars, Jupiter and Saturn
12. Sun, Mars, Venus and Saturn
13. Sun, Mercury, Venus and Saturn
14. Sun, Jupiter, Venus and Saturn
15. Moon, Mars, Mercury and Jupiter
16. Moon, Mars, Mercury and Venus
17. Moon, Mars, Mercury and Saturn
18. Moon, Mars, Jupiter and Venus
19. Moon, Mars, Jupiter and Saturn
20. Moon, Jupiter, Venus and Saturn
21. Mars, Mercury, Jupiter and Saturn
22. Mars, Mercury, Venus and Saturn

Five Planets

1. Sun, Moon, Mars, Mercury and Jupiter
2. Sun, Moon, Mars, Mercury and Venus
3. Sun, Moon, Mars, Mercury and Saturn
4. Sun, Moon, Mars, Jupiter and Venus
5. Sun, Moon, Mars, Venus and Saturn
6. Sun, Moon, Mercury, Venus and Saturn
7. Sun, Mars, Jupiter, Venus and Saturn
8. Moon, Mars, Mercury, Jupiter and Venus
9. Moon, Mars, Mercury, Jupiter and Saturn
10. Moon, Mars, Mercury, Venus and Saturn
11. Moon, Mars, Jupiter, Venus and Saturn
12. Mars, Mercury, Jupiter, Venus and Saturn

Six Planets

1. Sun, Moon, Mars, Mercury, Jupiter and Venus
2. Sun, Moon, Mars, Mercury, Jupiter and Saturn
3. Sun, Moon, Mars, Mercury, Venus and Saturn
4. Sun, Moon, Mars, Jupiter, Venus and Saturn
5. Sun, Moon, Mars, Jupiter, Venus and Saturn
6. Sun, Mars, Mercury, Jupiter, Venus and Saturn
7. Moon, Mars, Mercury, Jupiter, Venus and Saturn

The conjunction of four or more planets may show its effect on the material plane as described earlier, or it may lead to an ascetic life. Before deciding on which plane the conjunction will manifest, it is necessary to assess any planetary potential inclining the native to forego the pleasures of ordinary life, to willingly embrace an austere existence and sever all worldly attachments, to dedicate oneself to a hard and simple life and, above all, to attune one's mind and spirit to the pursuit of divine bliss. To judge all factors of a chart, we may refer our readers to our other book, *Hindu Predictive Astrology*. Here we shall simply offer some guidelines which should be followed to determine the potential for asceticism. A few yogas[2] leading to asceticism are given below:

Yogas for Asceticism

1. If the dispositor[3] of the Moon (a) aspects Saturn or (b) is aspected by Saturn and is not aspecting or aspected by any other planet.

2. If Saturn is not aspected by any other planet, but Saturn aspects the dispositor of the Moon.

The crux of (1) and (2) is that the dispositors of the Moon and Saturn should not be aspected by any other planet and the dispositor of the Moon should aspect Saturn or be aspected by it.

3. If the Moon occupies Saturn's drekkana,[4] and is also located in Saturn's or Mars' navamsha, and if such a Moon is aspected by Saturn.

To save our readers the job of calculation we shall give the degrees wherein the Moon will be in Saturn's drekkana and in Saturn's or Mars' navamsha.

---

2   In Sanskrit, 'yoga' means "union." Thus in mysticism it refers to union with God, while in Hindu astrology it refers to a "union" or combination of planets.

3   The dispositor of the Moon is the planet which rules the sign occupied by the Moon. This definition applies to all planets: i.e. if the Moon is in Capricorn its dispositor is Saturn; if Mars is in Taurus its dispositor is Venus.

4   The drekkana, like the navamsha, is one of the sixteen vargas or divisional charts; specifically, it represents division of each sign by three.

20° 00′–23° 20′ Gemini
10° 00′–13° 20′ Virgo
10° 00′–16° 40′ Libra
00° 00′–06° 40′ Capricorn
03° 20′–06° 40′ Aquarius

If the Moon is located in any of the above degrees (in the sidereal zodiac) and aspected by Saturn, it leads to asceticism. This is the view of Varaha Mihira.

According to Kalyan Varma, another classical author:

1. If the Moon is located in Saturn's drekkana and aspected by Mars and Saturn, it leads to asceticism. The following degrees in the sidereal zodiac constitute Saturn's drekkana:

20°–23° Taurus
20°–30° Gemini
10°–20° Virgo
10°–20° Libra
00°–10° Capricorn
00°–10° Aquarius

2. If the Moon is located in Mars' navamsha and is aspected by Saturn, it also leads to asceticism. The following degrees in the sidereal zodiac constitute the navamsha of Mars.

00° 00′–03° 20′ and 23° 20′–26° 40′ Aries
10° 00′–13° 20′ Taurus
03° 20′–06° 40′ and 20° 00′–23° 20′ Gemini
13° 00′–16° 40′ Cancer
23° 20′–26° 40′ Leo
10° 00′–03° 20′ Virgo
03° 20′–06° 40′ and 20° 00′–23° 20′ Libra
13° 00′–16° 40′ Scorpio
23° 20′–26° 40′ Sagittarius
10° 00′–13° 20′ Capricorn
03° 20′–06° 40′ and 20° 00′–23° 20′ Aquarius
13° 00′–16° 40′ Pisces

We are inclined to agree more with Varaha Mihira.

4. If the Ascendant is Cancer, Sagittarius or Pisces and aspected by Saturn with Jupiter in the Ninth house.

5. If Saturn is in the Ninth house and not aspected by any planet. (It may be aspected by the dispositor of the Moon. That is a plus factor and not a minus one.)

6. If the dispositor of the Moon is aspected by a combination of all the other planets.

7. If Saturn is in an angle and aspected by the dispositor of the Moon. This dispositor should be free from combustion.

8. If either the Sun, Moon or Jupiter is weak and in the First, Tenth or Twelfth house and aspected by a strong Saturn.

9. If the birth is in the bright fortnight, the Moon is strong in digital as well as on other counts, and such a Moon aspects a weak lord of the Ascendant.

In several of the above yogas, the aspect of Saturn plays an important role. We have, however, found that the conjunction of Saturn produces the same effect as his aspect.

It may be relevant to add here that we have observed in many nativities that these yogas do not lead to asceticism but that the person must, under pressure of circumstances, abdicate or renounce a high office, i.e. that of kingship, presidency or prime-ministership.

4

ASPECTS OF THE SUN,
MOON AND MARS

Just as the conjunction of two or more planets modifies their individual effects, so also do aspects. The ancient Sanskrit text *Jataka Deshamarga,* Chapter 10, verse 3, states:

"When malefics are endowed with strength and occupy benefic subdivisions,[1] they prove auspicious if they be aspected by benefics posited in benefic subdivisions. On the other hand, if benefics be devoid of strength, occupy malefic subdivisions, and are also aspected by malefics posited in malefic subdivisions, they generally prove baneful in their effects."

As a general principle a malefic should prove baneful in its effect while a benefic should confer a blessing, but the quality of influence is modified by the following factors:

    1. Strength or weakness of the planet.

    2. Whether the planet is in benefic or malefic subdivisions of a sign.

    3. Whether the planets aspecting the planet under consideration are benefics posited in benefic subdivisions or malefics posited in malefic subdivisions.

    4. Whether the aspecting planet itself is aspected by other planets, and whether these latter are strong or weak, benefic or malefic, lords of good houses or bad ones, well placed or ill placed.

Here our inquiry will be confined to point (3) above, i.e. the aspect. We will not, at present, consider the intricacies of subdivisions. Generally, ten subdivisions of a sign are taken into account. For these ten subdivisions, readers are referred to any standard astrological textbook. It would be too elaborate and outside the compass of this book to delineate the

---

1   The term "subdivisions" is equivalent to the Sanskrit word vargas, i.e. the harmonic divisions of each zodiacal sign. See footnote 1, Chapter 3, p. 53.

effects of planets aspecting other planets according to their placements in the subdivisions, so we shall confine ourselves here only to the aspects themselves, but we may state as a general proposition that if the aspecting planet is placed in benefic subdivisions the effect will be better. If, on the other hand, the aspecting planet is in malefic subdivisions, the good effects will be mitigated in some measure and the evil ones augmented.

All planets are considered to have a "full" aspect upon the house or sign which lies opposite their own position, i.e. in the seventh house from the planet's own place. Mars also fully aspects the fourth and eighth houses from its own place; Jupiter the fifth and ninth; and Saturn the third and tenth. With these exceptions, all other planets have *half* aspect on the fifth and ninth signs from their own positions, a *quarter* aspect on the third and tenth signs, and a *three-quarters* aspect on the fourth and eighth. The aspecting planet affects not only the *signs* or *houses* in these positions, but any *planets* which occupy those signs or houses.

In this book, the effects described are only for full aspects, but the readers may apply partial aspects also in proportion to their effect.

Example

♓	♈	♉	♊
♒			♋
♑			♌ ☉ ☽ ☿ ♀ ♂ ♃ ♄
♐	♏	♎	♍

The Sun, Moon, Mercury or Venus, if occupying Leo, will fully aspect Aquarius and the planets therein. Mars in Leo in the birth chart will fully aspect Scorpio, Aquarius, Pisces, and any planets occupying those signs. Jupiter in Leo will fully aspect Sagittarius, Aquarius, Aries, and planets therein. Saturn in Leo will fully aspect Libra, Aquarius, Taurus, and any planet occupying any of these signs.

ASPECTS OF THE SUN

When the Sun Aspects the Moon in

ARIES: The native is haughty in disposition, persevering, fond of engaging in disputes and controversies, but he has a benevolent attitude towards those who submit to him.

TAURUS: The native is very industrious and wealthy; he may gain from agriculture and may have a number of employees and cattle.

GEMINI: The native is religious, learned and wise. He has a comely appearance but is not wealthy. He is sorrowful.

CANCER: The native engages in government service but is devoid of wealth; not meritorious. He may be an administrator or a career military man, but he will undergo much stress and strain.

LEO: The native has conflicts with the government. He is very heroic and courageous and occupies a high position. He is famous but engaged in sinful acts.

VIRGO: The native may be employed in the revenue or finance department of the government; he is well renowned. He accepts the advice of others and performs noble deeds but is devoid of marrital happiness.

LIBRA: The native is sickly and has little stamina; he wanders aimlessly, is oppressed and devoid of luxuries of life. He has no sons or little happiness on their account. He is not rich.

SCORPIO: The native is rich and learned; he travels much. He is not popular and people are antagonistic to him.

SAGITTARIUS: The native attains a high position and is renowned for his heroic deeds. He has luxury goods and vehicles. He is rich and prosperous.

CAPRICORN: The native is proficient as an artisan or craftsman. He is in the employment of others. He does not have a well-groomed appearance and is not rich. He is sorrowful or melancholy.

AQUARIUS: The native is very chivalrous but is of uncouth appearance or dresses shabbily; he gains from agriculture or land, attains a good position in life and is religious.

PISCES: The native has luster and leads a comfortable life. He may become a military officer or have many employees under him. He is wealthy, strongly sexed and happy with his wife.

Readers will note that when two planets aspect each other, two sets of effects are generated, one due to the natural inherent qualities of the planets and the other due to their lordships. In Western astrology, oppositions and square aspects are considered evil, while sextiles and trines are considered good. Thus, if the lord of the Second is in a square or opposition to the lord of the Fifth, there may be loss of money due to speculation, children, pleasures, and love affairs (Fifth house affairs), but if the two lords — Second and Fifth — are in favorable aspect, there may be gain of money due to Fifth house affairs. That is the general principle. But not so in Hindu astrology. For example, the mutual aspect of the lords of the Ninth and the Eighth is evil, but between the lords of the Ninth and Tenth is good. In short, aspects between the lords of good houses — lords of angles and lords of trines — is good, while aspects of the lord of the Sixth, Eighth or Twelfth denigrates the good effects and produces evil ones.

Besides, in Hindu astrology there is no flat rule to judge the effects of aspects, because the previous paragraphs have shown that the quality of the Sun's aspect on the Moon differs from sign to sign according to the location of the Moon in various signs. This is a special feature of Hindu astrology. Generally, when we delineate the effect of aspects, it should be taken to mean the full aspects. It may be argued that we are justified in evaluating effects in proportion to the measure of the aspect. Thus, if the Sun has a 50% aspect on the Moon, we may ascribe 50% of the influence described for the Sun's aspect on the Moon. This argument sounds logical enough. But the convention and practice is to pinpoint the effect of the aspect only when there is a full aspect, and when a Hindu astrologer says the Moon is aspected by the Sun he means the full aspect only. In yogas also, only the full aspect is deemed effective.

When the Sun Aspects Mars in

ARIES OR SCORPIO: The native is wealthy, blessed with a wife and sons. He may occupy a position of authority where he may inflict punishment on the guilty. He is well renowned and generous.

TAURUS OR LIBRA: The native is of a fiery temperament; there is disharmony in his conjugal life. The native has a large number of opponents and is fond of visiting mountains and forests.

GEMINI OR VIRGO: The native is fond of mountains and forests. He has much stamina and is courageous. This aspect also confers learning and wealth.

CANCER: The native has much perseverance and is assertive. He may become a magistrate or a judge with powers to award punishment, but he suffers from bilious (i.e. Pitta) complaints.

LEO: The native owns a herd of cattle and is fond of outdoor life; he extends patronage to those who pay homage to him, has a number of friends, but is of fiery temperament.

SAGITTARIUS OR PISCES: The native has a comely appearance; he wants to live outside the bustle of the town. He is cruel but respected.

CAPRICORN OR AQUARIUS: The native is dark but very courageous. He has wealth, a wife, and sons. He is sharp-tempered and aggressive.

Since Mercury and the Sun are never more than twenty-eight degrees away from each other, Mercury can only be in the same sign as that occupied by the Sun or in the second or twelfth signs from the Sun. Since the two planets have no aspect when they are in the same sign or in the second and twelfth from each other, there can be no aspect between the Sun and Mercury. The effect of a Sun-Mercury conjunction has already been described earlier, and so we shall now take up the Sun's aspect on Jupiter.

When the Sun Aspects Jupiter in

ARIES OR SCORPIO: The native is religious, truthful in speech and very prosperous. He has much hair on his body. His son becomes very famous.

TAURUS OR LIBRA: The native owns a herd of cattle and has a number of employees. He is fond of traveling and has a large body. He is learned and wise and will occupy a high position.

GEMINI OR VIRGO: The native occupies a good position. He is the head of his village or town. He is wealthy, blessed with a wife and sons, and has a large family.

CANCER: The native is a leader of men and groups and becomes very famous. He is devoid of happiness, wife and wealth. In the latter part of life he becomes wealthy.

LEO: The native is liked by the gentry; he is well renowned, occupies a kingly position and is very wealthy and prosperous. He is courteous and very even-tempered.

SAGITTARIUS OR PISCES: The native is bereft of wealth and deserted by his relatives. He suffers mental anguish. He antagonizes the king by working against him.

CAPRICORN OR AQUARIUS: The native is intelligent and wise. He is very heroic and prosperous and leads a luxurious life. He occupies a lofty position and extends patronage to a large number of people.

The Sun and Venus are never more than forty-eight degrees apart, so Venus is always in the same sign as the Sun or in the second, third, eleventh or twelfth from him. Hence Venus can receive only a one-quarter aspect of the Sun, and since we are delineating the influence of full aspects, we shall move on to the Sun's aspect on Saturn.

When the Sun Aspects Saturn in

ARIES OR SCORPIO: The native may do well in agriculture, and he has a herd of cattle (buffaloes, cows, sheep and goats). He is industrious and engaged in work. He is prosperous.

TAURUS OR LIBRA: The native's body is very delicate, fine and soft. He speaks clearly and is learned. He is devoid of wealth and avails himself of the hospitality of others.

GEMINI OR VIRGO: The native is devoid of happiness and is in indigent circumstances; he has much physical forbearance and is persevering. He also has control over his temper and is religious.

CANCER: The native is separated from his father or mother at a young age and has to eat "coarse food." He is devoid of wealth, wife and happiness.

LEO: The native does not have a good body and he is devoid of wealth and happiness; his conduct is not good; he serves others. He is addicted to untruth, given to liquor, and leads an unhappy life.

SAGITTARIUS OR PISCES: The native begets sons with other peoples' wives. From his illegitimate sons he receives wealth, respect and renown.

CAPRICORN OR AQUARIUS: The native has to bear much physical hardship; he travels constantly but his wanderings and traveling yield little dividend. His appearance is not good; his health is failing and he does not have conjugal happiness. He is dependent upon others for his livelihood.

ASPECTS OF THE MOON

Whenever two planets conjoin together or fully aspect each other, there is an element of give and take. When two benefics like Mercury and Jupiter or Jupiter and the Moon fully aspect or conjoin each other, they mutually fortify each other and augment their inherent good qualities; but when a malefic and a benefic conjoin or fully aspect each other, the evil qualities of the malefic are reduced but the positive qualities of the inherent benefic may also suffer, in some measure, due to receiving the baneful aspect.

In this chapter, the delineation of the aspects is strictly on the basis of inherent qualities. But it is reiterated that while judging the conjunctions or aspects of planets, the lordships should also be considered. For example, a full aspect between the lord or a trine and the lord of an angle is always good, whatever the nature of the planets. It is good for the lord of the Ascendant to be aspected by the lord of a good house but unfavorable if he is aspected by the lord of an evil house.[2] The aspecting planet's location in a sign also affects its influence. It is not possible to give all the effects of planets in each of the twelve signs aspecting all the other planets in various signs, so we shall limit our explanation to the aspect of each planet on other planets in signs according to their rulership.

When the Moon Aspects the Sun in

ARIES OR SCORPIO: The native has a soft and attractive body; he is fond of damsels and they are fond of him; he has a number of servants and is inclined to charity and benevolence.

TAURUS OR LIBRA: The native is soft-spoken; a large number of damsels receive patronage from him; he is fond of dancing girls; he may gain money by water transport, goods brought across waters, or aqueous products — fish, pearls, etc.

---

2   The Sixth, Eighth and Twelfth are deemed evil houses.

GEMINI OR VIRGO: The native is tormented by his enemies and relations; he suffers much; he moves to a place other than his homeland and faces troubles there.

CANCER: The native gains money by trading in goods across waters or by dealing in aqueous products. He is of fixed determination but cruel, and occupies a very exalted position.

LEO: The native is intelligent and a favorite of the king. He has a good wife but suffers from phlegmatic diseases (i.e. an imbalance of Kapha. See footnote 1, Chapter 1, p. 17) .

SAGITTARIUS OR PISCES: The native has a good body, is of peaceful mind, and is happy. He is endowed with eloquence and intelligence. He is wealthy and occupies a high position.

CAPRICORN OR AQUARIUS: The native is clever in hiding his own thoughts and practicing deception on others. He has no fixity of mind. He loses wealth and happiness through contacts with women.

When the Moon Aspects Mars in

ARIES OR SCORPIO: The native suffers unhappiness in respect to his mother (either there is premature separation from the mother or not much love lost between mother and son). There are wounds or boils on the body; the native is devoid of friends and inimical to his own people; he is envious but fond of girls.

TAURUS OR LIBRA: The native may be inimical to his mother; he is neither even-tempered nor cooperative; he is attached to a number of women and is liked by them. The native is lacking in courage and boldness.

GEMINI OR VIRGO: The native may be in charge of a girl's hostel or may be their guardian; he may be employed in the king's household. He is good to look at and very courteous.

CANCER: The native occupies an administrative position where he awards punishment. He is bold, aggressive and persevering, but suffers from bilious diseases (diseases related to Pitta. See foonote 1, Chapter 1, p. 17).

LEO: The native may be prematurely separated from his mother or she may suffer in health. He is intelligent, has a solid body and gains renown. He may also gain through a female (his own wife or some other lady).

SAGITTARIUS OR PISCES: The native is intelligent and learned but restless and quarrelsome. He is antagonistic to the king (i.e. he may act in opposition to the government).

CAPRICORN OR AQUARIUS: Not an auspicious configuration in respect to the native's mother. The subject is fickle but of a generous disposition. His friendships are not firm and his wealth is fluctuating; he possesses jewelry.

When the Moon Aspects Mercury in

ARIES OR SCORPIO: The native is very attractive to women, but his conduct is not good. He is slovenly and engages himself in the service of others.

TAURUS OR LIBRA: The native is very reliable and wealthy. He enjoys good health and has a good family. He is religious and renowned. He occupies an exalted position.

GEMINI OR VIRGO: The native is sweet to look at but very talkative. He is devoted to learning and books but is quarrelsome. The native is successful in his undertakings.

CANCER: Much of the native's physical stamina is wasted due to congress with women. He leads an unhappy or sickly life due to women. He has little happiness.

LEO: The native has a handsome appearance; he is very clever, fond of poetry, dance, drama, arts and crafts. He dresses well and is wealthy.

SAGITTARIUS OR PISCES: The native has a tender body; he is a good writer. His conduct as a householder is approved by gentle-folk. He is wealthy and reliable and leads a luxurious life.

CAPRICORN OR AQUARIUS: The native is wealthy and prosperous. He gains money through aqueous products or goods transported across water or by shipping, boating, irrigation, tanks, dams etc., or by merchandise. He may also gain money by dealing in spirits, liquors, fermented products or roots (things grown under the earth, such as potatoes). He is not fond of traveling and is cowardly.

When the Moon Aspects Jupiter in

ARIES OR SCORPIO: The native is well versed in history, drama and poetry, and is possessed of jewelry. He is intelligent and learned and receives favors from ladies. He occupies a high position.

TAURUS OR LIBRA: The native is sweet, receives much affection from his mother, and is beloved of many damsels. He enjoys life very much.

GEMINI OR VIRGO: The native is very handsome and rich. He is happy and has a wife and sons. The native's conduct is much praised by gentle-folk. His mother is very fond of him.

CANCER: The native is very wealthy. He has a lustrous personality. He is endowed with a number of vehicles and luxury items. His mother is a person of status. He occupies a high position in life.

LEO: The native is a highly moral person with a great deal of self-control; he is very courteous and even-tempered. He becomes rich and wealthy due to his wife (her good stars or good influence). He has an attractive personality but dresses in a slovenly manner.

SAGITTARIUS OR PISCES: The native has many luxury items. He is wealthy, is held in high esteem, and is proud. He is very attractive to women.

CAPRICORN OR AQUARIUS: The native is a gentleman of good conduct. He is devoted to his parents. He is courteous and even-tempered. He comes of a good family and is very religious.

It will be observed that the effects described above for the Moon's aspect on Jupiter are generally good. The Moon's attributes, however, differ according to whether he is waning or waxing. The Moon with more than ten digits (in the bright half of the month) will show very good effects, while the same Moon's aspect would not be so good if he is waning (in the dark half of the month) or the digits are less than five. The Moon's general strength — the sign he is in, his dispositor, location, etc. — also has an influence. The more benefic and stronger the Moon, the better results he will produce. If the Moon is in a malefic's sign, hemmed in between malefics and aspected by malefics, he will be too weak to show any marked good results. These remarks apply not only to the Moon's aspect on Jupiter, but to his other aspects and conjunctions also.

When the Moon Aspects Venus in

ARIES OR SCORPIO: The native's wife may not come from a high-status family, or the native may have liaisons with low-class women; he is very active but of changeable disposition; he may become accused in a case.

TAURUS OR LIBRA: The native comes from a high-status family but he suffers in respect to his sons; he has many luxury items; his conduct is good; he is agreeable to look at and leads a comfortable life.

GEMINI OR VIRGO: The native has dark hair and black eyes; he has a tender body and an attractive appearance; he enjoys the "comforts of the bed"[3] and vehicles and leads a prosperous life.

CANCER: The native has a stepmother, or the native's father may have a liaison with some other woman. His first child is a daughter, then several sons are born. He is attractive and soft and leads a happy life.

LEO: The native has a stepmother; he is wealthy but suffers on account of his own wife or other women. This suffering may be caused on account of his own frustration due to unfulfilled desires or to circumstances created by them. He is fickle-minded.

SAGITTARIUS OR PISCES: The native enjoys good food, drink, and all kinds of luxuries in abundance. He has extraordinary stamina; he occupies a chief position under the king and is well renowned.

CAPRICORN OR AQUARIUS: The native has moral stamina and is assertive; he is very courageous. He has a good body and an attractive personality.

The Moon and Venus are both benefics. Venus, however, is a planet of sex and luxury, and these attributes are generally strengthened by the Moon's aspect. It should, however, not be lost sight of that an opposition of the Moon and Venus from the Second and Eighth houses or from the Sixth and Twelfth impairs eyesight.

When the Moon Aspects Saturn in

ARIES OR SCORPIO: The native is active in body but fickle in mind; he is attached to low-class women who are unattractive (our

---

3 This is a euphemism used by ancient authors to indicate the pleasures of sex.

experience is that some of them may also be older than the native). He is devoid of wealth and happiness.

TAURUS OR LIBRA: The native is loved by the ladies and derives strength and money from them. He has a large family. His work is appreciated by the government and he is rewarded.

GEMINI OR VIRGO: The native wins much approbation, respect and money from ladies, and runs errands for them. He occupies a high position. He has a smooth and lustrous body.

CANCER: This is an inauspicious configuration in respect to happiness from the mother. The mother may fall ill after the native's birth or there may be premature separation from her. Also the native does not get on well with his brothers and sisters. But he is wealthy.

LEO: The native has an abundance of wealth and jewelry; he is very famous and enjoys the company of young women. He receives favors from the government.

SAGITTARIUS OR PISCES: The native has a wife, sons and wealth; he is cool-headed and courteous; he may have two names, both equally popular. There may be premature separation from the mother or the lack of an affectionate relationship with her.

CAPRICORN OR AQUARIUS: The native is fickle-minded, untruthful in speech and sinful in conduct. He courts misery by traveling; he earns wealth by his own effort. This is not a good configuration in respect to happiness on the mother's account.

ASPECTS OF MARS

When two planets are in the seventh sign from each other, there is a full aspect between them. But besides having a full aspect on the seventh, Mars also has full aspect on the fourth and eighth houses from its own. Thus if Mars is in Capricorn and the Sun in Leo, Mars will have full aspect on the Sun but the Sun will not aspect Mars. So only the effect of the aspect of Mars to the Sun will be made manifest.

When evaluating the effects of Mars' aspect on various planets, not only should the sign position of the aspected planet be taken into account, but the sign position of Mars as well. Mars in Cancer (i.e. its fall) cannot generate the same effect as Mars in Capricorn (exaltation) or Aries (its own sign). Nor should the lordships be lost sight of. For someone with a Scorpio Ascendant the mutual full aspect between Mars and Jupiter will be a configuration of the lords of the First, Second, Fifth, and Sixth. That will be very good because no blemish will be attached to Mars due to his ownership of the Sixth, thanks to the fact that he also owns the Ascendant. But for Virgo Ascendants, a configuration of Mars and Jupiter will involve the lords of the Third, Fourth, Seventh and Eighth, which would be particularly evil for Fourth and Seventh house affairs.

Another important factor is the location of the lord of any given house in any of the twelve houses. For example, the lord of the First house may occupy any of the houses. The effects arising from any house lord's position in any given house must also be considered. In order to arrive at a full and complete picture of any horoscope, we have to synthesize the various factors by adding up all the influences, favorable and otherwise, then arrive at a conclusion. What has been stated here applies not only to Mars, but to all the other planets. The principle remains the same. Now let us take up the effect of Mars' aspect on various planets according to the sign occupied by the aspected planet.

When Mars Aspects the Sun in

ARIES OR SCORPIO: The native is very courageous and puts up a good fight; he is cruel; his eyes and the soles of his feet are reddish. He is endowed with much heroism and strength.

TAURUS OR LIBRA: The native is fond of battle and possesses an heroic luster. He acquires wealth and fame by dint of his courage and aggressive nature, but he is restless.

GEMINI OR VIRGO: The native is apprehensive of his enemy but quarrelsome; he does not win laurels in battle but suffers humiliation and is distressed and humbled. He is a little shy.

CANCER: The native suffers from dissipatory or inflammatory diseases, e.g. fistula, cancer, phthisis; there is no love between himself and his relations. He is distressed and is a back-biter.

LEO: The native is very courageous and occupies an eminent position. He is industrious but at times furious. He accomplishes difficult tasks by sheer force of will and courage, but he is attached to other people's wives.

SAGITTARIUS OR PISCES: The native has a fiery temper and wins laurels in battle. He speaks very clearly and forcefully. He is wealthy and endowed with happiness.

CAPRICORN OR AQUARIUS: The native is distressed due to enemies, diseases, and quarrels on other people's account; his body wears many a scar. He is restless.

When Mars Aspects the Moon in

ARIES: The native suffers from eye trouble and dental ailments; he may also suffer from weapons, poison and "heating diseases,"[4] or be troubled by evil spirits. (One may interpret this literally, i.e. as "possession" or a "haunting;" or one may favor a more psychological interpretation.) But he occupies a good position as head of an institution or region.

TAURUS: The native is over-sexed and forsakes his wife and friends for the sake of other women. He is adored by young women, but this configuration is evil in respect to the mother. There may be premature separation from her or not much love lost between mother and son.

GEMINI: The native is very learned and courageous; he is endowed with good looks, wealth, vehicles and happiness.

CANCER: The native is courageous, endearing and clever, but of questionable health — there may be an infirmity in some limb or a chronic ailment. This configuration is evil in respect to the mother; she may suffer illness or premature demise, or the native may not be on affectionate terms with her.

LEO: The native is of fiery temper; he may be a policeman or military officer, or take up a profession involving metal or fire. He becomes an eminent person and is endowed with wife, sons, wealth, and vehicles; he has employees.

VIRGO: The native suffers in respect to his mother; otherwise this is a good aspect. He is educated, persevering, clever in mechanics and artisanship, rich and famous.

LIBRA: The native is intelligent but short tempered, mean and thievish. He enjoys others' wives and a life of luxury, but suffers from diseases of the eyes.

SCORPIO: The native has indomitable courage and never suffers defeat. He has extraordinary perseverance and remains unruffled

---

4   i.e. diseases connected with Pitta. See footnote 1, Chapter 1, p. 17.

despite all difficulties. He is endowed with wealth but is gluttonous.

SAGITTARIUS: The native is the head of an army or regiment, or the head of an institution. He is good-looking and wealthy. He serves exceedingly well and has helpful subordinates. He attains much fame.

CAPRICORN: The native has an attractive appearance, is very wealthy and generous; he has many luxury items and vehicles, but possesses a fiery temper.

AQUARIUS: The native is truthful in speech but unmanageable and inflexible. He is separated from his mother and the senior members of his family. He is employed by other people and inclined to be indolent. He is devoid of wealth.

PISCES: The native is sinful; courageous but oppressed. He is devoid of happiness. His mother is not "a good woman."

It will be observed that the aspect of Mars on the Moon makes one bold and courageous. Because fortune favors the brave, the native becomes successful in his undertakings and earns name and fame; wealth and riches follow as natural corollaries. But the Moon is also the significator for the mother, and when Mars, a natural malefic, aspects the Moon, the prospects for a good relationship with one's mother are low. All the principles given in this book are based on ancient Sanskrit texts. It is frequently stated that when the Moon is in a particular sign the native may lose his mother prematurely, whereas if the Moon is in another sign the native's mother may be wicked or of loose morals. But the aspect of Mars on the Moon is a common factor in both cases, and the subtle distinctions — i.e. between loss and alienation — are merely providing a glimpse of what the ancients have stated in their wisdom and experience. There are innumerable Sanskrit works on Hindu astrology, many of which are not available in English, and our intent is to familiarize our readers with the astrological aphorisms enunciated in these ancient texts.

When Mars Aspects Mercury in

ARIES OR SCORPIO: The native is fond of lies and is quarrelsome, but he is learned and speaks well. He is courageous and a favorite of the king. He is very wealthy.

TAURUS OR LIBRA: The native's health is impaired due to a chronic disease; he faces difficulties and is distressed due to humiliation at the hands of the government. He does not enjoy life.

GEMINI OR VIRGO: The native is highly intelligent and serves the king, but his body may have scars of wounds or there may be an infirmity in some limb. He is a slovenly dresser, but very popular nonetheless.

CANCER: The native is not very learned but talks too much. He speaks sweetly, but is fond of lies and has a scheming nature. He has thievish instincts.

LEO: The native has scars or wounds on his body or suffers from some infirmity in a limb. His morals, business ethics, and general conduct are filled with distress, and he is afflicted with sorrow. He is not clever but has attractive mannerisms. His virility is impaired.

SAGITTARIUS OR PISCES: The native writes well or is skilled in calligraphy. He becomes the head of a group of people — i.e. a union, whether of thieves or citizens or, as the classical texts say, of "dwellers in the forest." The idea is that the native occupies the head position in some organization, the type of organization depending upon other factors.

CAPRICORN OR AQUARIUS: The native has very gentle looks but is flippant and eloquent in speech. He is a little bashful and indolent. He leads a comfortable life.

When Mars Aspects Jupiter in

ARIES OR SCORPIO: The native is courteous and diplomatic but does not have a happy marriage or helpful servants. He engages in the service of the king and is valorous and aggressive, but without wealth.

TAURUS OR LIBRA: The native is wise, valorous and wealthy. He serves the king. He is much loved by young damsels.

GEMINI OR VIRGO: The native is rich and always procures pleasures. He is popular and commands esteem, but there is an infirmity in some limb.

CANCER: The native marries at an early age or has a young wife. He is intelligent and possesses much jewelry. He is very heroic and has scars on his body. He is rich.

LEO: The native is cruel and aggressive in temperament; he performs great deeds; he is truthful and devoted to his seniors and religious preceptors. He leads a clean life and is very efficient.

SAGITTARIUS OR PISCES: The native has a mutilated body due to injuries (inflicted in a battle or accident). He is cruel and has a propensity to hurt others, to whom he causes distress.

CAPRICORN OR AQUARIUS: The native is very heroic and may be in the army. He is famous, of good conduct, and much respected. He is proud and assertive. He dresses well.

When Mars Aspects Venus in

ARIES OR SCORPIO: The native works in a subordinate capacity, running errands for others; he is devoid of wealth, happiness and respect. His actions are low and not commendable.

TAURUS OR LIBRA: The native's wife is ill-tempered; he does not have domestic felicity, and neglects his wife for the sake of another woman. He is over-sexed.

GEMINI OR VIRGO: The native has a comely appearance but is very amorous; he squanders his wealth for the sake of a young damsel.

CANCER: The native is rich and proficient in many arts. He has an attractive personality. His relations prosper due to his good offices, but he suffers distress on account of a woman or women.

LEO: The native occupies an important post under the king (in the government). He has a charming personality and gains riches due to a young lady (his wife or some other woman). He has liaisons with other's wives.

SAGITTARIUS OR PISCES: The native is much envied by women; he is wealthy. He has uncommon experiences of happiness as well as distress. He has a large herd of cattle (i.e. wealth).

CAPRICORN OR AQUARIUS: The native is sickly; his wife dies prematurely or gives rise to great distress. He works hard at physical labor but is happy in the latter part of life.

It will be observed that Mars-Venus aspects make one over-sexed, and that various corollaries follow. Mars represents sexual desire in a woman, while Venus represents the same in a man. The color of Mars is red like the menstrual discharge of a female while the color of Venus is white like semen.

In Greek mythology, Ouranos, the god of the sky, was both the son and lover of Gaia, Mother Earth. Ouranos hated his children and confined some of them beneath the earth in Tartarus, in consequence of which he was castrated and dethroned by his son Cronus at the instigation of Gaia. Out of the drops of his blood sprang many monstrous creatures, but from his semen which fell into the sea sprang Aphrodite or Venus, the goddess of love.

In the *Iliad,* Charis is described as the wife of Hephaestus, but in the *Odyssey,* it is Aphrodite who appears as the wife of the lame god of smithcraft. And though the *Iliad* calls her the daughter of Zeus and Dione, Hesiod tells us how she sprang from the foam of the sea after Ouranos' castration (her name means "born of the sea foam"). She was the mother of the love god Eros (from whence the word "erotic"), and was identified with the springtime by the Romans and by medieval Latin poets. Never a faithful wife, she took Ares, the god of war (Latin: Mars) as her lover.

In Hinduism, Venus is also identified with the goddess of love — Lakshmi, who, like the Greek Aphrodite, is born from the great ocean, in this case during he mythic "churning of the ocean" by gods and demons. And just as Eros or Cupid is the son of Aphrodite, the Hindu Cupid is the son of the goddess Lakshmi. This cupid is called Makara Ketan (having a flag with an emblem of a crocodile flying on his chariot) and also Mina Ketan (having a flag with an emblem of a fish flying on his chariot). Why? Because Mars, presiding over sex in women, is exalted in Capricorn (Makara, the crocodile) while Venus, presiding over sex in men, is exalted in Pisces (Mina, the fish). The conjunction or full aspect of Mars and Venus generally leads to an unsatisfactory or stormy sex life.

When Mars Aspects Saturn in

ARIES OR SCORPIO: The native is intent on killing (men, animal, birds, etc.); he is cruel and a ringleader of thieves (smugglers, tax-evaders, black marketeers); he is fond of women, wine and meat. But he is famous.

TAURUS OR LIBRA: The native is wealthy and has a number of people around him. He is very talkative and well versed in the details of battles, but a renegade from active warfare.

GEMINI OR VIRGO: The native excels as a wrestler; he becomes famous but has to put up with much physical labor and may suffer infirmity in some limb. His discretion is overcome by his emotions.

CANCER: The native is wealthy, but his wealth is appropriated by the government. He suffers from an infirmity of some limb.

LEO: The native wanders or is a frequent traveler, but such traveling does not pay dividends; his actions are not commendable.

He is fond of living in forts, forests and hills. He has thievish tendencies. He is devoid of happiness on account of his wife and sons.

SAGITTARIUS OR PISCES: The native suffers from diseases arising out of an imbalance of wind, such as rheumatism or gout (imbalance of Vata; see footnote 1, Chapter 1, p. 17); he is mean and his actions are sinful; he is envious of other people.

CAPRICORN OR AQUARIUS: The native is heroic and aggressive. He becomes famous due to his extraordinary qualities. He occupies an eminent position as leader of men. He is sharp and courageous.

5
ASPECTS OF MERCURY
AND JUPITER

MERCURY

As Mercury and Venus are always near the Sun, Mercury can have no aspect on the Sun except conjunction, but conjunction is not treated as an aspect in Hindu astrology as it is in the Western system. Mercury can have, at most, a sixty-degree or sextile aspect on Venus, but here we are dealing with full aspects, so we shall confine ourselves to the aspects of Mercury on the Moon, Mars, Jupiter and Saturn.

Mercury is a very mutable planet. Ancient texts state that if Mercury is conjoined with natural benefics he should be treated as a benefic, while if he combines with a natural malefic he becomes malefic. By nature, Mercury is inherently benefic. His occupancy of a house enhances its good effects. His aspect upon any house likewise augments the benefic influences pertaining to that house.

When two planets aspect each other, as stated earlier, there is mutual give and take. But due to the volatile nature of Mercury, he takes more than he gives. In other words, when Mercury and another planet fully aspect each other, Mercury is affected more than he affects. Thus, when appraising Mercury's aspect on another planet never neglect to determine how Mercury himself has been affected by the other planet.

When Mercury Aspects the Moon in

ARIES: The native is well versed in the various branches of learning; he speaks well and may be a good poet. He is agreeable and earns much fame.

TAURUS: The native is endowed with many extraordinary qualities. He is intelligent, does good to others, is cheerful and speaks well.

GEMINI: The native occupies an eminent position and is obeyed. He is very persevering and undefeated. He is very clever in making money.

CANCER: The native has a steady intelligence; he is diplomatic, occupies the position of a minister and is endowed with all kinds of comforts. He is rich and has a wife and sons.

LEO: The native has feminine traits; he is attractive to women and generally under their influence; he is under the command of a lady, either his own wife or some other woman. He has luxuries and is wealthy and happy.

VIRGO: The native is well versed in poetry and astrology. He is victorious in controversies. He is very clever and efficient.

LIBRA: The native is well versed in the fine arts. He has a great deal of money and owns granaries. He speaks well and sweetly. He is learned and very famous.

SCORPIO: The native is not clever and his speech is not well considered; he may have twins (children). The native is a connoisseur of singing and is diplomatic.

SAGITTARIUS: The native has very good skin. He has a number of servants. He is well versed in astrology and arts and crafts. If other planetary combinations point to asceticism, he may take to a religious order which advocates nudity.[1]

CAPRICORN: The native is fickle, lacks intelligence, and lives abroad. He may suffer a premature separation from his wife. He is sharp in temper, without wealth and happiness.

AQUARIUS: The native is well versed in the arts of sex, a connoisseur of singing and beloved of women. He has a good body and wealth.

PISCES: The native is surrounded by a number of exceptional women. He occupies an eminent position and is happy.

Thus we observe that Mercury's aspect on the Moon is generally good except when the Moon is in Scorpio or Capricorn. The Moon and Mercury are both inherently benefic and it is no wonder that good effects are generated due to the aspect of one benefic on another.

We may, however, add that the Moon and Mercury in the seventh house from each other will be particularly productive of good effects when

---

1   The reference here is to those wandering sadhus of India who give up all worldly possessions, even their clothing.

the two planets become the lords of a trine and an angle. For example, when Libra is rising the Moon becomes the lord of the Tenth house and Mercury the lord of the Ninth. When Pisces is rising, the Moon becomes the lord of the Fifth and Mercury the lord of two angles, the Fourth and Seventh. For Gemini or Virgo Ascendants, the Moon will be the lord of the Second and Eleventh respectively, and an aspect between the lord of the First and Second or between the lords of the First and Eleventh is good for the acquisition of wealth.

When Mercury Aspects Mars in

ARIES OR SCORPIO: The native is clever in appropriating other peoples' wealth; he is untruthful and addicted to sex. The native creates much antagonism and often has liaisons with "unchaste" women.

TAURUS OR LIBRA: The native speaks much and is quarrelsome. He is learned and has a soft body. He has little wealth and few sons.

GEMINI OR VIRGO: The native is clever in mathematics, poetry and calligraphy. He speaks much and sweetly but is not truthful in his speech. He may work as an intermediary or agent. He is capable of bearing much physical stress, strain and hardship.

CANCER: The native is uncouth or unclean and his conduct is sinful. He has a limited family and his family members shun him. The native is shameless.

LEO: The native is clever in arts and crafts and fond of poetry. He is avaricious and not even tempered. He is very clever and capable.

SAGITTARIUS OR PISCES: The native has a good memory and is clever. He is very learned and efficient. He is well versed in arts and crafts.

CAPRICORN OR AQUARIUS: The native is fond of traveling, is discontented, and does not have much stamina. He is devoid of wealth. He is a hypocrite and irreligious.

Readers will observe how the effects of Mercury's aspects change dramatically with different locations of Mars. When Sagittarius or Pisces is the Ascendant, a mutual aspect between these two planets will be very good because it will be a mutual aspect between the lords of an angle and a trine. When Gemini or Virgo rises, Mars will be the lord of the Sixth and Eleventh or Third and Eighth respectively, and as the houses owned by Mars are not good the general effect of a mutual aspect between the two planets will not be good either.

When Cancer or Leo is rising, Mars becomes the lord of two good houses, but the aspect between Mercury and Mars will be better when Leo is rising because it is an aspect between the lords of the Fourth and Ninth and Second and Eleventh. But with Cancer rising, Mercury will be the lord of the Third and Twelfth, which is not so good.

When Mercury Aspects Jupiter in

ARIES OR SCORPIO: The native is untruthful in speech; he cheats and is clever in finding flaws in others. He is given to hypocrisy. He is courteous, serves well, and is grateful to those who do good to him.

TAURUS OR LIBRA: The native is sweet, intelligent, clever and wealthy and has many admirable qualities. He has a pleasing personality and is courteous, well-bred and good tempered. He enjoys many material comforts.

GEMINI OR VIRGO: The native is well versed in astrology and may be an original author. He has wives and sons. (When polygamy was prevalent in India, it was considered a mark of good fortune to have more than one wife.) He has excellent powers of expression and can present his case in many different ways.

CANCER: The native has a number of good relations and friends; he is wealthy; he does not indulge in sinful acts but may be quarrelsome. He occupies a responsible position as a counselor or adviser.

LEO: The native is learned, particularly in architectural sciences. He speaks endearingly. He has many virtuous qualities and occupies a senior position as a counselor or minister.

SAGITTARIUS OR PISCES: The native is endowed with sons, wealth, prosperity and happiness. He occupies a highly respectable position such as that of a minister. He is popular and much loved.

CAPRICORN OR AQUARIUS: The native has many fine qualities; he is wealthy and has a number of vehicles. He has many friends and is well renowned. He is amorous in disposition.

Both Mercury and Jupiter are planets which preside over intelligence and learning, but there is a subtle difference between the spheres over which they hold sway. Mercury indicates quickness in grasping or understanding, an intelligent appreciation, discrimination and balance while Jupiter denotes wisdom, depth and profundity. Mercury is quick and volatile and presides over the communications network of the human nervous system, while Jupiter, a more ponderous planet, helps in storing up knowledge and learning. Mercury is wit and speech; Jupiter is depth of knowledge. Dispersion is the characteristic of Mercury, accumulation that of Jupiter. Mercury governs expression while Jupiter presides over innate solidarity. It is when the best traits of both planets are present in a chart that a native can be truly learned, for Mercury will help him at the receiving or transmitting end while Jupiter will assist him to build up a reservoir of knowledge. A person with a good Mercury and a bad Jupiter may be able to impress others with his scintillating speech and activity but will lack in depth of learning and wisdom. A man with a good Jupiter and a bad Mercury may be a scholar of great erudition but will be wanting in the art of expression, either in speech or in writing.

When Mercury Aspects Saturn in

ARIES OR SCORPIO: The native is untruthful, given to irreligious acts, and has a thievish disposition; he is a glutton. He is devoid of happiness or material luxuries.

TAURUS OR LIBRA: The native is jocular and given to mirth; he serves women or runs errands for them; he loses his potency early in life. He is of a low disposition.

GEMINI OR VIRGO: The native is well versed in the arts of singing and dancing. He is wealthy and clever in battle or military strategy. He is also efficient in the arts and crafts, and generally a capable person.

CANCER: The native is cruel and very talkative; he is victorious over his enemies. His actions are good but bear the hallmarks of hypocrisy.

LEO: The native indulges in wicked acts; he is indolent and without wealth, uncouth in appearance and humble. He runs errands for women or performs the household duties of a woman.

SAGITTARIUS OR PISCES: The native is equal to a king, leading a happy and comfortable life. He is a great scholar. He is gentle and of good appearance, wealthy and respected.

CAPRICORN OR AQUARIUS: The native has "tamasic" qualities (anger, avarice, envy, enmity). He is capable of putting up with much physical hardship. He is well-groomed and endowed with knowledge, but has little money. He is much praised.

JUPITER

Thus we observe that the effects of Mercury's aspect change according to Saturn's location in the various signs. We shall now take up Jupiter's aspects. It may not be an exaggeration to state that Jupiter's aspect is perhaps the best to improve good effects and even to transform bad ones into more positive potentialities as far as possible. But if the inherent location of the aspected planet is bad, how far can Jupiter go in changing it into a good one? A congenitally sick or deformed person will not show the same reaction to vitamins and tonics as will a healthy person.

When Jupiter Aspects the Sun in

ARIES OR SCORPIO: The native is very wealthy and generous; he is a king's minister or occupies some equally high rank where he awards punishment (e.g. he is a magistrate or judge). He is a person of a high order.

TAURUS OR LIBRA: The native has a number of friends and enemies. He is a minister to the king or occupies an equally eminent position. He is easily pleased and is always intent on work. He has beautiful eyes and a comely appearance.

GEMINI OR VIRGO: The native is well versed in various branches of learning and speaks exhaustively on various subjects. He may live abroad; he becomes successful as an agent or ambassador. He is of fiery temper and intoxicated either with pride or due to liquor.

CANCER: The native is a person of a high order; he may be a commander, a chief or even a king, and very famous. He is well versed in the fine arts.

LEO: The native constructs temples, tanks and gardens. He has much stamina but prefers a life of seclusion. He is wise and highly intelligent.

SAGITTARIUS OR PISCES: The native is very learned; he is always seen moving about in the king's palaces. He has horses and elephants and is very wealthy. He occupies a kingly position.

CAPRICORN OR AQUARIUS: The native's deeds are praiseworthy. He extends patronage to all. He is very intelligent and attains much fame. He applies himself arduously to the undertakings in hand.

Jupiter and the Sun are natural friends: a well placed Sun, if aspected by Jupiter, becomes better still. For Aries, Cancer, Leo, Scorpio and Sagittarius Ascendants the aspects of Jupiter will be at their best.

When Jupiter Aspects the Moon in

ARIES: The native is wealthy and has a number of servants. He is a king's minister or the head of a section of the army.

TAURUS: The native is devoted to his parents; he has good and fast friends and happiness in respect to his wife and sons. He is very capable, religious and famous.

GEMINI: The native has an attractive appearance and is very truthful in speech. He is a master of many branches of learning and eloquent. He is famous and well respected.

CANCER: The native occupies a kingly position and has royal qualities and attributes. He lives happily at home and has a good wife and conjugal happiness. He is courteous, diplomatic and courageous.

LEO: The native belongs to a good family and is the scion of an eminent house. He is very learned and endowed with many good qualities. The native occupies a kingly position.

VIRGO: The native accepts good advice. He has a number of good relations. He leads a comfortable life and engages in government service.

LIBRA: The native is respected everywhere. He is clever in the purchase and sale of goods, particularly jewelry and utensils.

SCORPIO: The native is actively engaged in his work. He is wealthy but envied. He has good looks.

SAGITTARIUS: The native is wealthy and religious and occupies a position analogous to that of a minister. He has an excellent physique and is happy.

CAPRICORN: The native is blessed with a wife, sons and friends. He is endowed with royal qualities and occupies a kingly position.

AQUARIUS: The native enjoys beautiful damsels; he has a number of houses and villages, lands and orchards. He is a good and gentle person.

PISCES: The native occupies a prominent position among chiefs. He has a soft body and is very rich. He has a delicate and pleasing appearance and is surrounded by young damsels.

In judging the effects of Jupiter on the Moon, due consideration should be paid to the strength of the Moon and the strength of the Moon's dispositor, as well as to the strength of Jupiter. Let us clarify this point with a few examples. The Moon is in Capricorn: if it is a waxing Moon, the good effects shown by the Moon therein will be stronger than if the Moon is waning. Similarly, if Saturn, the dispositor of the Moon, is weak, good effects will not manifest in so large a measure.

Jupiter in Taurus, Cancer or Virgo would all fully aspect the Moon in Capricorn. But Jupiter exalted in Cancer will show far better results on the Moon than Jupiter in Taurus or Virgo, where he is in his enemies' signs.

The strength of the sign in which the Moon is located, apart from digital strength, will be an additional factor. (Elaborate rules have been given in Hindu astrology to ascertain the digital strength of a planet in a particular sign, but the details involve cumbersome calculations and thus are not explained here.) We shall now take up the effects of Jupiter's aspect on Mars.

When Jupiter Aspects Mars in

ARIES OR SCORPIO: The native has a handsome appearance; he is sweet and intelligent, beloved by his parents and wealthy. He occupies a unique position and has many luxuries.

TAURUS OR LIBRA: The native is a connoisseur of singing and music; he prospers and is a favorite of his relations. He is clean.

GEMINI OR VIRGO: The native excels as an agent or ambassador and may visit foreign countries in that capacity. He may engage in government service. He is very capable in various undertakings and eventually comes into the limelight.

CANCER: The native is very learned and becomes famous; he may become a king's minister; he is much praised but devoid of the luxuries of life.

LEO: The native has a clear mind and a discriminating intelligence; he is very learned and may be a professor, or he may be on the staff of a king and hold charge of a section the army.

SAGITTARIUS OR PISCES: The native is wealthy and is never subdued by his enemies. He engages in physical exercise, but he is devoid of wife and happiness.

CAPRICORN OR AQUARIUS: The native has a number of good relations and is endowed with various kingly qualities. He applies himself diligently to whatever he commences. He is not handsome but is long-lived.

Thus we observe how Jupiter's aspect tones down the inflammatory Mars. Due to the aspect of Jupiter, the energizing qualities of Mars flow in constructive channels. If Mars is in the fifth or ninth position from Jupiter, Jupiter alone will have its full aspect on Mars, but if Mars and Jupiter are in the seventh from each other, they will aspect each other and the aspect of Mars on Jupiter should also be taken into consideration.

* * *

When Jupiter aspects Mercury, it makes the native very intelligent. Without going into the sign positions of Mercury, the *Horasara* of Prithuyashas states (Chapter 20, Shloka 7): "When Jupiter has full aspect on Mercury, the native becomes a king whose orders will be implicitly obeyed by other princes."

We believe that the good effects of the combination are here glorified to the extent of exaggeration, but what no one will hesitate to concede is that the native will be highly intelligent and his sound advice accepted by even the highest people. Though the effects of aspects in Hindu astrology have been described primarily on the basis of the full aspect, we have observed in a number of nativities that even the sextile aspect of Jupiter to Mercury, when exact, makes one highly intelligent, particularly if Mercury is applying to Jupiter. Even where Jupiter aspects Mercury by trine or opposition, the effects will be better if Mercury applies to Jupiter within a close orb. The principle of degree-to-degree aspects is not followed in Hindu astrology, where aspects are considered simply from sign to sign. But if in addition to the sign-to-sign aspect there is also a close relationship by degree, the aspect will no doubt become stronger for the good. Degree aspects are a principle of Western astrology, and though we should not seek to impose rules which contradict our own basic principles we should be intellectually liberal enough to borrow any guidelines which supplement rather than supplant.

When Jupiter Aspects Mercury in

ARIES OR SCORPIO: The native has a smooth but hairy body. He has an abundance of hair on his head. He occupies a position of command. He is very wealthy and leads a comfortable life.

TAURUS OR LIBRA: The native is learned and intelligent. He accepts the good advice tendered by others. He occupies a prominent position in his own country, town, union, or assemblage of people (the degree of prominence depends on the general strength of the nativity). He will be famous.

GEMINI OR VIRGO: The native has a handsome appearance, is generous, has a large family and possesses many luxury items. He is chivalrous and becomes chief among ministers or a king.

CANCER: The native is intelligent and has a good memory. He is prosperous, much loved by people, and a favorite of kings. He is well versed in several branches of learning.

LEO: The native has a soft and elegant body; he is intelligent and learned. He has great eloquence in speech. He has a number of servants, subordinates, and vehicles.

SAGITTARIUS OR PISCES: The native excels as a writer, is the minister or treasurer of a king, and is well-versed in the sciences. He has intelligence and his family commands respect. He has a good appearance.

CAPRICORN OR AQUARIUS: The native is wealthy and owns granaries. He leads a comfortable life. He receives homage from his village, town, or union. He attains fame.

It will be observed that very good effects are described for Jupiter's aspect on Mercury regardless of the sign occupied by the latter. The reason is threefold. First, both are benefics. Second, the two planets are allied in presiding over intelligence, learning, wealth, etc. Thirdly, both are karakas (significators) for the Tenth house, which governs activity, position, honor and respect.

Obviously Mercury in Gemini or Virgo aspected by Jupiter in Sagittarius or Pisces respectively will be extremely strong for the good, since both planets will be in their own houses. Though the texts delineate the same effects for Mercury in Sagittarius or Pisces (the two signs owned by Jupiter), readers should not ignore the fact that Mercury will be debilitated in Pisces and therefore naturally weaker.

We take this opportunity to explain that if any planet is aspected by its dispositor, it is considered a very good feature. Suppose planet 'A' is in a sign owned by planet 'B'; the dispositor of 'A' will be 'B'. In the present example, if Mercury is in Sagittarius or Pisces, the two signs owned by Jupiter, then Jupiter will be the dispositor of Mercury. The *Phala Deepika*, an ancient Sanskrit astrological text from South India, states (Chapter VII, verse 28):

> When a planet is in debilitation but aspected by the lord of the sign in which he is posited,[2] a yoga is formed which will make the native a ruler and a famous one. And, in the above yoga, if the debilitated planet is in a good house, there is no doubt that the native will become a prominent ruler.

This dictum actually concerns cancellation of the evil effects of a debilitated planet. But the spirit of the above rule is that if a planet is weak or in affliction, that weakness or affliction is reduced by his dispositor's aspect on it. The author further states that if a planet is in a good house, the aspect of his dispositor makes him yield very good results. We shall now return to our original format and discuss Jupiter's aspect on Venus.

* * *

It should be remembered that Jupiter and Venus are both benefics — of the two, Jupiter is the greater benefic. Some features are common to both. Both planets, if strong, confer wealth and happiness. Jupiter is the significator for wealth while Venus is the significator for worldly luxuries and comforts. But Jupiter stands for knowledge, wisdom and peace of mind, while Venus symbolizes romance, pleasure, and the desires of the flesh. Jupiter is masculine, Venus is feminine. Jupiter presides over sons, religious preceptors and the like, and Venus over wives, damsels, courtesans, etc. Both are expansive planets, but Jupiter is a significator of procreation while Venus rules pleasure and poetry. Jupiter's love is divine, that of Venus mundane. Jupiter represents the fruit of trees while Venus stands for the flowers. Jupiter is the seed, Venus the pollen. Jupiter commands, Venus cooperates. Jupiter makes one wise, Venus makes one

---

2   The term *location* refers to a planet occuying a particular sign or degree. When we refer to its occupying a particular house, the term is *position* or *posited*.

amiable. Jupiter regulates fat in the human body, Venus governs the sex glands and the semen. Despite these differences, both are essentially benefic (though Jupiter's aspect is stronger for good than that of Venus). But one point must be emphasized: technically the two planets are enemies to each other.[3]

When Jupiter Aspects Venus in

ARIES OR SCORPIO: The native has a good, large body and attractive eyes; he has a good and generous wife; he has several sons.

TAURUS OR LIBRA: The native is blessed as regards his wife and sons and is fortunate in respect to houses and vehicles. He is engaged in good work.

GEMINI OR VIRGO: The native leads a very happy life but has humility. He excels in making duplicates of original pieces. He is learned, an erudite scholar, and capable of being a good teacher.

CANCER: The native is a favorite of the king; he is blessed with sons, relations, friends and servants. He is wealthy and in command, owning vehicles and luxuries.

LEO: The native marries more than once or has several major love affairs. He rises to the position of minister to the king or some equal rank. He is wealthy and has servants and vehicles.

SAGITTARIUS OR PISCES: The native is blessed with a good wife and sons. He leads a very happy life. He has cattle, horses and elephants and is wealthy.

CAPRICORN OR AQUARIUS: The native has a good wife; he is a connoisseur of songs and music. He has a soft and elegant body. He is fond of fine apparel, flowers and scents.

✳ ✳ ✳

We shall now deal with Jupiter's aspect on Saturn. These planets have certain common features. Both are large and very distant from the Sun. Both give depth, and their benefits (or otherwise) mature in old age. Both lend stability, but while Jupiter expands, Saturn contracts. Both, when

3   See Footnote 6, Chapter 1, p. 29.

well placed, tend to make one religious, but while Jupiter favors rituals and devotion, Saturn inclines to a nihilistic philosophy of asceticism. Jupiter elevates the mind but Saturn depresses. Jupiter is generous in giving, Saturn is tight-fisted. It is generally observed that Jupiter's aspect helps in mitigating the evil qualities of Saturn. It would, however, be relevant to note that it would be better for Jupiter to aspect Saturn with a trine, for in that case the native, while having the full benefit of Jupiter's aspect over Saturn, will not have the ill effect of Saturn's aspect on Jupiter, for Jupiter's aspect on the fifth and ninth houses from itself is full while Saturn's trine aspect in Hindu astrology is only half strength.

When Jupiter Aspects Saturn in

ARIES OR SCORPIO: The native is endowed with wealth and happiness and prospers. He becomes a minister to the king and occupies the foremost position on the government staff.

TAURUS OR LIBRA: The native devotes himself to other people's work and shares their joys and sorrows. He is actively engaged in work and is bountiful in giving to others.

GEMINI OR VIRGO: The native is liked by the gentry. He is endowed with many fine qualities. He is trusted in royal circles. He has secret deposits of wealth.

CANCER: The native owns fields and houses; he has a number of friends and sons. He is blessed with a wife, wealth and jewelry.

LEO: The native is the foremost member of his village, town or union. He is blessed with sons. He is sweet-tempered and courteous. He is relied upon by people.

SAGITTARIUS OR PISCES: No impediments or adverse circumstances cross the native's path; he may become the commander of an army, a minister, or even a king. He occupies an exalted position.

CAPRICORN OR AQUARIUS: The native has many admirable qualities. He is long-lived and does not suffer ill health. He works for the sovereign. He attains a very high position.

Here it will be observed how Jupiter, by shedding his golden light on Saturn, transforms the dark heavy planet into a benign one. Normally Saturn is dreaded in any house, unless he is in his own sign. But it should be noted that when Saturn is well placed, he brings infinite good. One important effect of Saturn is especially relevant here. The planet is a distant and heavy one and represents old age. People who have a strong, well aspected Saturn generally pass the latter years of their lives comfortably, but people with an afflicted Saturn, especially in the Fourth house, pass their old age in want and privation. Saturn, if afflicted in the First house, makes one's childhood miserable due to both ill health and want of financial resources.

Alan Leo has written that Saturn in the Tenth raises a person very high in life but then drops him down to suffer ignominy and disgrace. This view, however, is not shared by all Hindu astrologers. The positive or negative effects of Saturn in the Tenth would depend largely on the sign he tenants and the houses he rules. For Cancer, as lord of the Eighth in the Tenth, he may cause the premature demise of the father. But for a Capricorn Ascendant, Saturn would be the lord of the First and Second and exalted in the Tenth. Hence he would do very well. For Aries and Taurus Ascendants he would be in his own sign in the Tenth, thus also powerful for good. Thus we should not tar Saturn in the Tenth with too sweeping a brush.

6

ASPECTS OF VENUS

AND SATURN

VENUS

We shall now deal with the aspects of Venus on other planets. Obviously, Venus can never fully aspect the Sun or Mercury, for it is never that distant from them. So we shall take up the aspects of Venus on the Moon, Mars, Jupiter and Saturn.

When Venus Aspects the Moon in

ARIES: The native is good-looking, blessed with wealth and sons; he possesses jewelry and enjoys life; he has an excellent wife.

TAURUS: The native has jewelry, vehicles and houses. He enjoys "the comforts of the bed." He has fine apparel and many luxuries — flowers, scents, good furniture, elegant vehicles — in short, he has more than the normal quota of the enjoyments of life.

GEMINI: The native has an excellent wife; he possesses and uses precious stones and costly jewelry, flowers, fine clothes and vehicles. He has many luxury items.

CANCER: The native is blessed with money and gold and has fine fashionable apparel. He possesses jewelry and the enjoyment of young damsels. He has very attractive looks and is fond of courtesans.

LEO: The native is wealthy and enjoys women very much. He is in a position of subordination to a lady. He is learned and well-versed in the amorous arts, but suffers in health.

VIRGO: The native has several wives (or, in the present-day context, enjoys several women). He is wealthy and enjoys many luxury items. He prospers daily.

LIBRA: The native excels in diplomacy and in achieving his ends by various means. He has good health and an elegant body.

He is good-looking and has well-proportioned limbs. He is rich and learned.

SCORPIO: The native is intelligent but proud; he has good looks. He is wealthy and has expensive vehicles. He leads a luxurious life, but much of his stamina is seeped away due to women.

SAGITTARIUS: The native has a good wife, friends and sons. He is blessed with sons and is wealthy. He is elegant and good-looking. He is very amorous.

CAPRICORN: The native has affairs with other peoples' wives. He is wealthy and has the luxury of using scents, flowers and jewelry. He owns vehicles. He may suffer in respect to his sons and his reputation.

AQUARIUS: The native's conduct is low; he is devoid of friends and sons; he does not have much courage. He does not have a happy marriage. He has little happiness. He indulges in sinful acts and is condemned by his religious preceptors.

PISCES: The native is sweet-tempered and fond of amorous alliances, singing and dancing. He very much attracts the members of the opposite sex and is liked by them.

Venus is primarily the planet of love and pleasure, beauty and aesthetics, harmony in color and form, sex and singing, melody and amiability. It denotes cooperation, luxuries, fine apparel, jewelry, scents, vehicles or conveyances, comforts and residences, also houses of recreation and enjoyment. Venus and the Moon both preside over the element of water. In Hindu astrology as in Hindu philosophy, earth, water, fire, air and ether are regarded as the basic elements, each successive one being finer than the preceding one. So when Venus aspects the Moon the various inherent qualities of Venus come to the fore. Of course, the effect differs according to the location of the Moon in the various signs of the zodiac.

We shall now take up the effects of Venus aspecting Mars.

When Venus Aspects Mars in

ARIES OR SCORPIO: The native suffers confinement or imprisonment due to a woman; he loses wealth and earns money due to feminine influence.

TAURUS OR LIBRA: The native becomes a military officer or policital minister. He is a favorite of the king and his name is well renowned. He leads a comfortable life.

GEMINI OR VIRGO: The native has a comely appearance and is prosperous. He enjoys good food and fine apparel. He works in subordination to a woman or runs errands for a lady or ladies.

CANCER: The native is mentally agitated due to the company of a woman and causes connected with women; he is insulted and loses money.

LEO: The native enjoys several women and various luxuries; he is very endearing to women, cheerful and always youthful.

SAGITTARIUS OR PISCES: The native is generous and possesses paintings, jewelry and other pieces of art. He is much inclined to sex and enjoyment; he has an attractive appearance.

CAPRICORN OR AQUARIUS: The native is endowed with all the paraphernalia of luxury; he is engaged in supporting damsels; he is also quarrelsome.

Thus we observe that as Mars represents the sex instinct in a female and Venus the same factor in a male, the aspect of Venus over Mars brings into play the latent qualities of sex and enjoyment. As Mars and Saturn are both malefic, Mars' aspect on Venus in a sign of Saturn, while endowing one with luxuries, gives him a quarrelsome temperament as well.

When Venus Aspects Jupiter in

ARIES OR SCORPIO: The native is well endowed with the comforts of home, the bed, apparel, scents, flowers, garlands, jewelry, damsels and luxuries, but he is a coward at heart.

TAURUS OR LIBRA: The native has a very delicate and attractive body; he is very wealthy; he has the enjoyment of other people's jewelry; he puts on fine and fashionable apparel and has ample comforts of the bed; he is allergic to uncleanliness.

GEMINI OR VIRGO: The native is very attractive to women and wins their hearts; he enjoys conjugal happiness and has a luxurious wardrobe; he is engaged in the work of temples, etc.

CANCER: The native has several wives (in ancient India to have more than one wife was considered a token of enjoyment and good fortune); he is very rich and possesses jewelry and other luxury articles; he has an attractive appearance and leads a happy life.

LEO: The native is much honored by the king; he has much stamina; he is good-looking and beloved of the womenfolk.

SAGITTARIUS OR PISCES: The native has an attractive appearance; he is free from faults, is intelligent, learned, wealthy and happy; the goddess of fortune smiles upon him and he is long-lived.

CAPRICORN OR AQUARIUS: The native is well endowed with food, drink and other luxury items. He puts on fine apparel and jewelry; he has comforts such as a fine residence, furniture, vehicles and good women (i.e. the pleasures of sex).

Venus presides over luxuries and enjoyment, while Jupiter presides over wealth and learning, so the aspect of Venus on Jupiter is always good. In Hindu astrology Jupiter and Venus are enemies, but the fact that both are benefics makes up for that enmity and, in the final analysis, Venus aspecting Jupiter is good. For the finer shades of difference in assessing the aspect of Venus on Jupiter, we have to take into account their respective ownerships also (i.e. of which houses they are the lords).

For example, for a Virgo Ascendant Venus would be the lord of the Second and Ninth and Jupiter the lord of the Fourth and Seventh; as such the lord of a trine (Venus) aspecting Jupiter as lord of two angles (the Fourth and Seventh) would be conducive to far greater good fortune than usual, for it would be a sambandha[1] between the lords of a trine and two angles. But if the mahadasha[2] of Jupiter and antardasha of Venus or the mahadasha of Venus and antardasha of Jupiter occur in old age, this period may well be fatal to the native, because for Virgo Ascendant Venus as lord of the Second house and Jupiter as lord of the Seventh would also be marakas,[3] and their maraka propensities would be increased if either planet were located in the Second or Seventh. For a Gemini Ascendant also, Venus becomes the lord of a trine (i.e. the Fifth house, with no blemish attached to its ownership of the Twelfth because the Fifth house is such an auspicious one) and Jupiter the lord of two angles, and as such

---

1   A Sanskrit word including conjunction and mutual full aspect. Sambandha literrlly means joining up or connection.

2   Mahadasha means "major direction" while antardasha means "minor direction". Both refer to cycles of planetary rulership. For details see Chapters 13-15 of *Hindu Predictive Astrology*.

3   A technical term in Hindu astrology signifying planets causing death.

their sambandha would be conducive to good fortune, but due to ownership of the Seventh house Jupiter would have maraka propensities also.

For Aries, Cancer and Scorpio Ascendants as well, the full aspect of
Venus on Jupiter will give rise to sambandha between the lords of a trine
and an angle and as such is good for prosperity, but Venus will be a maraka
for Aries rising and Jupiter for Scorpio. For Capricorn and Aquarius,
Venus owning the Fifth and Tenth or Fourth and Ninth respectively will
be wholly favorable, without any trace of inauspicious ownership. As such
it will be a yogakaraka.[4] But for Capricorn Ascending, Jupiter will own
the Third and Twelfth, hence not so good, and for Aquarius Jupiter owning
the Second and Eleventh will be conducive to wealth but a maraka due to
its ownership of the Second house.

For Taurus and Libra Ascendants, Venus is auspicious because he
owns the rising sign, but Jupiter rules the Eighth and Eleventh or the Third
and Sixth, which is not good. Similarly, for Sagittarius and Pisces Ascendants Jupiter owns two good houses, but Venus owning the Sixth and
Eleventh or the Third and Eighth respectively is not favorable.

For Leo, Venus owns one good house (the Tenth) but one evil house
(the Third), and Jupiter's ownership of a trine (the Fifth) is good but his
lordship of the Eighth (the worst house in any chart, unless the lord of the
Eighth owns the First house as well or is posited in the Eighth) is not, and
thus the full aspect between the two planets would confer no rajayoga.

The above discussion is intended to cultivate in the minds of the
readers the habit of not arriving at snap judgments by considering the
effects of the aspects simply in terms of a planet's inherent qualities, but
to probe more deeply into the influences generated by their respective
ownerships also.

We shall now take up the delineations of the ancient texts concerning
the aspect of Venus on Saturn. The two planets are mutual friends. When
Venus owns the ascending sign, Saturn owns two good houses. For Taurus
Ascendant, Saturn owns the Ninth and Tenth and becomes a yogakaraka.
Similarly, when Libra is ascending Saturn becomes the lord of the Fourth
(an angle) and Fifth (a trine) and is again a yogakaraka.

---

4   A planet owning both a trine and an angle and thus causing extremely
    good results.

Saturn is the owner of two signs — Capricorn and Aquarius. When Capricorn rises, Venus becomes a yogakaraka by owning the Fifth and Tenth, and when Aquarius rises Venus becomes the lord of the Fourth and Ninth. Thus one of these planets always becomes a yogakaraka when a sign owned by the other is rising. As regards the ownership of houses Venus and Saturn have affinity. But as far as their inherent traits are concerned, they are poles asunder. Venus governs adornment, affection, amusement and amiability, while Saturn signifies austerity, application, ailments and asceticism. Venus is expansive, Saturn the planet of limitation. Venus bestows pleasure, Saturn denies it; Venus is courteous, Saturn reserved. Venus will promote all that is beautiful, and in Saturn's train come sadness and sorrow. Venus is delightful, elegant and entertaining. Saturn is depressing, devitalizing and gloomy. Venus kindles joy in the heart, like the sight of a young damsel. Saturn produces awe like a stoic saint. If Venus is youthful vigor, Saturn is senile despondency. Venus is amorously sportive, Saturn a hard taskmaster. Thus their fundamental natures differ.

When Venus Aspects Saturn in

ARIES OR SCORPIO: The native is very active but not often of attractive appearance. He is attached to other people's wives and dancing girls. He is not endowed with the luxuries of life.

TAURUS OR LIBRA: The native has much stamina and is a favorite of the king. He possesses jewelry. He derives pleasure from wine and women.

GEMINI OR VIRGO: The native is clever in the art of decoration; he may run beauty salons for ladies and is often favored by women. He may also excel in yoga.

CANCER: The native is born in a prestigious family but is devoid of good looks and the pleasures of life. He is also devoid of comforts and happiness.

LEO: The native is good-looking but women are inimical to him. His progress is slow but he is wealthy and happy. He has a good end (i.e. he is rich in old age).

SAGITTARIUS OR PISCES: The native is fond of forests and mountains; he may be an adopted child or have two mothers and fathers (the biological parent and a godparent of some kind). He is busily engaged in work.

CAPRICORN OR AQUARIUS: The native is good-looking and wealthy. He leads a happy life and enjoys whatever pleasures present themselves. He is attached to other people's wives.

SATURN

We shall now deal with Saturn's aspects on the other planets. As Saturn fully aspects planets in the third, seventh and tenth houses from itself, it may be that Saturn fully aspects a planet while the other planet does not reciprocate the aspect. For example, if Saturn is in Aries, he will fully aspect any planets in Gemini, Libra and Capricorn, but a planet in Gemini or Capricorn will not fully aspect Saturn in Aries (except Mars in Capricorn, who will fully aspect Saturn in Aries because Mars, in addition to the seventh, also aspects the fourth and eighth signs from himself).

Conversely, Mars in Virgo will fully aspect Saturn in Aries but Saturn will not aspect Mars. Jupiter in Leo or Sagittarius will fully aspect Saturn in Aries, but Saturn will not aspect Jupiter. But when Saturn fully aspects a planet and that planet also aspects Saturn, two different sets of influences are generated, one due to Saturn's aspect and the other due to the aspect of the other planet on Saturn. The two must be synthesized to arrive at a genuine interpretation of the influence.

When Saturn Aspects the Sun in

ARIES OR SCORPIO: The native lacks intelligence; he is careless in work; he suffers ill health.

TAURUS OR LIBRA: The native's conduct is low; he is lazy and indolent, poor and not good-tempered; he suffers from some chronic disease; he is attached to or passes his time in the company of a woman older than himself.

GEMINI OR VIRGO: The native has many servants or subordinates but is always agitated in mind; he is always engaged in supporting a number of his relations. He is very cunning.

CANCER: The native's intelligence runs in a crooked channel; his actions are of the same kind (e.g. he appropriates other people's money and property). He is a back-biter, and he suffers from ailments arising out of an imbalance of wind (vata) and phlegm (kapha).

LEO: The native is very intent on sabotaging the efforts of others and is successful in such actions; he causes distress to others; he may lose potency early in life.

SAGITTARIUS OR PISCES: The native is unclean; he wants to maintain himself at others' cost; he is attached to low people, and fond of sport with quadrupeds (such as horse racing).

CAPRICORN OR AQUARIUS: The native overpowers and destroys his enemies; he is respected by the king and prospers thereby.

The Sun and Saturn are enemies and, naturally, the aspect of Saturn on this luminary is not good. But when Aries or Taurus is rising the mutual full aspect between the Sun and Saturn gives rise to a sambandha between the lord of a trine and an angle, and as such is good. There will also be a qualitatiave difference in the aspect according to the sign tenanted by Saturn. Whenever Saturn — or, for that matter, any planet — aspects another planet, certain general factors should be given due consideration:

1. The sign occupied by the planet making the aspect

2. The houses ruled by the planet making the aspect

3. The sign occupied by the planet receiving the aspect

4. The houses ruled by the planet receiving the aspect

5. The inherent nature of the planet receiving the aspect

6. The inherent attributes of the planet making the aspect

7. The house occupied by the planet making the aspect

8. The house occupied by the planet receiving the aspect, including various permutations and combinations which will give rise to many different locations and positions and which it is impossible to discuss in any one book.

The ancients have given delineations on the basis of factors 3, 5 and 6 above. The rest is left to the reader's own intelligence and discrimination. As a matter of fact, the aspect or aspects which the aspecting planet himself receives will also materially affect his aspect on other planets. For example, suppose Saturn in Sagittarius is aspecting the Sun. Now if Saturn himself is being fully aspected by Jupiter, the quality of Saturn's aspect will be much improved. On the other hand, if Saturn in Sagittarius in the First house is aspected by Mars, the quality of Saturn's aspect will suffer.

Having invited the attention of the readers to these subtle shades of difference, we shall return to considering the basic character of Saturn's aspects.

When Saturn Aspects the Moon in

ARIES: The native is hated and disliked and is inimical to others; he suffers much; he has an uncouth appearance; he is poor and indigent and does not speak truth.

TAURUS: The native is devoid of wealth and happiness; damsels are inimical to him. This is not a good aspect for the health or longevity of the native's mother, but he will have sons, relatives and friends. According to one view, if the Moon is in the first fifteen degrees of Taurus and aspected by Saturn it is evil for the native's mother, but if the Moon is in the latter half of Taurus and aspected by Saturn it is evil for the native's father.

GEMINI: The native is devoid of relations, wealth, happiness, luxuries and the company of young damsels. He suffers poverty and people are inimical to him.

CANCER: The native is devoid of happiness; he wanders aimlessly; he is poor, fond of falsehood, and his conduct is sinful; he is a low character; this aspect curtails happiness in respect to his mother.

LEO: The native labors; he may follow agricultural pursuits; he is without wealth, devoid of female company and bereft of happiness. He is a person of a mean order; he speaks untruth; he may be in charge of a fort or work as a guard.

VIRGO: The native does not have a strong memory; he is poor and unhappy; he is without a mother (or maternal happiness); he is under the influence of a damsel; women enjoy his wealth.

LIBRA: The native is rich and wealthy; he speaks sweetly; he has vehicles; he is much inclined to sex; he is bereft of happiness.

SCORPIO: The native comes from a lower-class family; he is devoid of wealth and is miserly; he suffers from some chronic disease; he is not truthful; his conduct is of a low order.

SAGITTARIUS: The native's speech is good and sweet and endearing; he is gentle and very learned. He is well bred.

CAPRICORN: The native is rich but lazy and indolent; he has a slovenly appearance; there is much cupidity in him and he is attached to others' wives. He is untruthful.

AQUARIUS: The native has coarse nails and rough hair on his body; he is of uncouth appearance, wicked, and attached to others' wives; he is not religious but he is rich and owns real estate.

PISCES: The native is restless. This is not a good aspect for maternal happiness. He is devoid of intelligence, wife and sons. He is attached to a low, unattractive woman.

Thus we observe that except when the Moon is in Libra or Sagittarius, the aspect of Saturn upon it is unfavorable. Again and again, it is emphasized that this aspect is not good for maternal happiness, which means that the native's mother may die early or there is not much love between mother and son.

The Moon is a significator of the mother, and, as Saturn is the most malefic of planets, his aspect impairs maternal happiness. The Moon is a very receptive planet and also governs the emotions; thus Saturn's aspect on the Moon has a very depressing, gloomy and melancholy effect on the mind. The Moon also signifies wealth. In Hindu mythology the Moon has been described as the brother of Lakshmi, the goddess of wealth, because both emerged from the ocean. This is a mythological representation of the fact that the Moon and the goddess of wealth both have a predominance of the element of water. In Hindu philosophy, water is treated as an element, not as a compound of oxygen and hydrogen. The consanguinity of the Moon and the goddess of wealth makes the Moon a significator for riches and splendor, and when the Moon is aspected by Saturn (except when the Moon is in Libra, Saturn's sign of exaltation, or in Sagittarius) the native's wealth is curtailed.

We shall now take up Saturn's aspect on Mars. Saturn becomes debilitated in a sign of Mars but Mars becomes exalted in a sign owned by Saturn. Saturn is neutral to Mars but Mars is an enemy of Saturn. Both are malefic, but they represent two poles of the same malefic nature — Mars representing the hot, quick and fiery end, Saturn representing the cold, slow and terminating end. Mars kills by expanding and bloating; Saturn takes its toll by contracting, concentrating and extinguishing. Mars antagonizes openly but Saturn undermines with malevolence. Mars is destructive, damaging and disruptive; Saturn brings about disintegration, delay and deterioration. Both are annihilating; only their methods and manners differ.

When Saturn Aspects Mars in

ARIES OR SCORPIO: The native is courageous in putting down thieves but, generally speaking, he lacks stamina; he is bereft of close relations: he is attached to another person's wife and maintains her or spends money on her.

GEMINI OR VIRGO: The native is engaged in some work connected with mines, forts, mountains or agricultural work. He is very valorous but has a slovenly appearance. He is poor and suffers sorrow.

TAURUS OR LIBRA: The native is happy, renowned, wealthy and learned, having relations and friends; he is the head of a village, town, or a union of people.

CANCER: The native has a very elegant body and his actions are analogous to those of a prince; he gains money by water transport (the import-export business in a modern context).

LEO: The native has the appearance of an aged person; he is without wealth; he visits other people's houses or resides there; he is fond of traveling; he is sorrowful.

SAGITTARIUS OR PISCES: The native does not have a good body, (i.e. his health may suffer or his physical appearance may not be good); he is fond of strife and battle; he wanders aimlessly; he follows another religion and is sinful and bereft of happiness.

CAPRICORN OR AQUARIUS: The native is intelligent and learned, courageous in warfare, very rich and rises to a high position; he has many children but damsels are inimical to him; he is bereft of happiness.

Thus we observe that good effects are described only when Mars is in the signs of Venus or Saturn and is aspected by Saturn.

✳ ✳ ✳

We shall now take up Saturn's aspect on Mercury. Here it is relevant to observe that while the Moon governs the emotions or the emotional mind Mercury governs the intelligence, and when the Moon and Mercury are both afflicted by Saturn the native may suffer from mental illness, lunacy, loss of memory, schizophrenia, etc. If Mercury and Saturn are well placed and rule good houses one may have powers of deep thinking and concentration and may excel in philosophy or the sciences, for Mercury presides over intelligence and Saturn over depth. If Mercury, in addition to being aspected by Saturn, is also aspected by good planets like Jupiter, one may excel in studies and mental pursuits.

Saturn's aspect on Mercury will also impart artfulness, dexterity and ability — which may become cunning if the birth chart is of a low order, or tact and diplomacy in better nativities. Saturn's aspect certainly bestows the capacity to conceal one's own thoughts — which may be used to good or bad purpose, depending upon other factors in the chart.

When Saturn Aspects Mercury in

ARIES OR SCORPIO: The native suffers many sorrows. He is fierce and intent upon killing others; he is bereft of friends and relations.

TAURUS OR LIBRA: The native is devoid of happiness and suffers sorrows on account of relations; he has an uncouth and slovenly appearance and suffers from chronic ill health. This aspect causes a lot of calamities.

GEMINI OR VIRGO: The native rises gradually in life and his efforts end in success. He is courteous and surrounded with luxury goods.

CANCER: The native is a hypocrite and indulges in sinful acts; he is devoid of good qualities and suffers imprisonment. His brothers and religious preceptors do not like him.

LEO: The native has a dry and large body; he perspires much, emitting a foul smell. The native does not have the comforts of life; he suffers many sorrows; he does not have an attractive personality.

SAGITTARIUS OR PISCES: The native is fond of forts and forests; he is a glutton, has a very slovenly appearance, and is inclined to be wicked. All his efforts to achieve an objective end in frustration.

CAPRICORN OR AQUARIUS: The native indulges in sinful acts; he works hard but is very poor. He is humble and very sorrowful.

It will be observed that only when Mercury is in his own sign and aspected by Saturn does he generate a positive influence; otherwise the result of Saturn's aspect on Mercury is evil. Some of the Saturnine attributes are austerity, affliction, fear, callousness, contraction, jealousy, malevolence, maliciousness, a secretive nature, sinful acts, worry, weariness, depression, destruction, grief, and gloom. No wonder he causes such dismal effects.

∗ ∗ ∗

We shall now take up the aspects of Saturn on Jupiter. Generally speaking, when Jupiter and Saturn are in mutual aspect Jupiter's aspect mitigates the evil traits of Saturn, but, in return, Saturn's aspect on Jupiter hampers the good effects of the latter planet.

When Saturn Aspects Jupiter in

ARIES OR SCORPIO: The native is sharp (in temper), courageous, avaricious and slovenly. He generally has the approbation of others and is successful in his endeavors but has fickle friends and sons.

TAURUS OR LIBRA: The native is intelligent and learned; he owns wealth and granaries and is a chief man in his village or town. But he is not attractive in appearance; he is slovenly and does not have joy regarding his wife.

GEMINI OR VIRGO: The native has an attractive personality; he is a leader of his village, union, town, or of the country.

CANCER: The native occupies a distinguished position in his village, town or the army; he talks much and owns many items. In old age, he enjoys a life of luxury.

LEO: The native experiences much enjoyment with fine damsels. He is eloquent and speaks much but sweetly. He is sharp (in temper) and devoid of happiness. He may become a good painter or possess paintings of artistic value.

SAGITTARIUS OR PISCES: The native, though good-looking, dresses in slovenly fashion; he is poor or humble, and condemned by the people of his village, town or union. He is devoid of happiness and enjoyment and is irreligious.

CAPRICORN OR AQUARIUS: The native owns cattle and has a number of servants. He is very learned and follows a very lucrative vocation. He rises to an eminent position and enjoys life.

Thus we observe that when Jupiter is in signs owned by Mercury, the Moon or Saturn and is aspected by Saturn, good effects are predicted. But to emphasize how the aspect of a malefic on a planet may denigrate its good effects, note the delineation for Saturn's aspect on Jupiter in Sagittarius or Pisces — his own signs — and receiving the full aspect of Saturn. Normally very good effects should be attributed to Jupiter in these signs, particularly if he is in an angle or trine, but we have seen above what havoc Saturn plays when he aspects Jupiter in Sagittarius or Pisces.

We shall now take up Saturn's aspect on Venus, which is the last in the series.

When Saturn Aspects Venus in

ARIES OR SCORPIO: The native is indolent, very slovenly in appearance, wanders aimlessly, and serves a person of the same temperament as himself; he has thievish tendencies.

TAURUS OR LIBRA: The native has little money and little happiness; his temper is not good and he is the husband of a low woman (or he may be attached to low women). He suffers from some chronic disease.

GEMINI OR VIRGO: The native leads a life of grief; he is defeated and overpowered by others; he is very fickle and inimical to others. He is stupid.

CANCER: The native is fallen (due to low conduct), fickle and poor. He does not have a well-groomed appearance; he is devoid of the comforts of life; he is under the influence of his wife (or some other woman).

LEO: The native occupies a very exalted position and is renowned; he has wealth and vehicles; he has good looks but is sorrowful; he is attached to a widow (or may marry a widow).

SAGITTARIUS OR PISCES: The native has an attractive personality; he is always wealthy, happy and in command of many luxuries. He leads a happy and comfortable life.

CAPRICORN OR AQUARIUS: The native is rich; he has a number of attendants and vehicles; he has many luxury goods. He has a dark but attractive personality. However, he dresses in a slovenly fashion.

Thus ends the delineation of the aspects of planets upon other planets according to the latter's locations in various signs. These chapters dealing with conjunctions and aspects of planets have not been presented with the intention that readers should follow them implicitly, but to acquaint them with what has been written on the subject in the ancient texts. As the number of Sanskrit scholars — particularly those familiar with astrological literature — is limited, it is useful to compile what the ancients, in their wisdom, thought and laid down to guide future generations. As far as the present writer is aware, no modern book on Hindu astrology gives such detailed delineations of conjunctions and aspects, covering the entire field. And unless readers who wish to understand the essence of the subject can become acquainted with the ancient writings, their knowledge is likely to remain incomplete.

One more point which affects astrological judgments is that the lord of any particular house will show specific effects according to its occupation of a particular house. This effect must naturally be blended with its sign position. Saturn in the Ninth in Libra will be much different from Saturn in the Ninth in Aries. Another factor is planetary rulership. For an Aries Ascendant, Saturn in the Ninth as lord of the Tenth and Eleventh will be different from Saturn in the Ninth as lord of the Seventh and Eighth when Cancer is the Ascendant.

7
THE NINTH
HOUSE

Of all the houses, the Ninth is the most important, because upon it depends one's general good luck and prosperity. So we are devoting a separate chapter to this house and delineating the effect of conjunctions in the Ninth house, as well as of Jupiter in the Ninth and aspected by one or more planets.

CONJUNCTIONS OF TWO PLANETS

SUN AND MOON: Good-looking but not long-lived; suffers from diseases of the eye; wealthy but fond of quarreling.

SUN AND MARS: Bold, aggressive and furious; intent upon quarreling; a favorite of the king but suffering distress in many ways.

SUN AND MERCURY: Clever and capable; has many enemies and meets much opposition; suffers distress and from various diseases.

SUN AND JUPITER: Long-lived; of good conduct and occupying a high position; very bold and courageous; is himself very wealthy and adds to his father's prosperity.

SUN AND VENUS: Enjoys flowers, scents, clothes and jewelry, but his body is sickly.

SUN AND SATURN: Not long-lived; suffers from diseases of the eye; is wealthy but quarrelsome; his father suffers from ill health.

MOON AND MARS: Increase in good luck and prosperity; a luxurious life, but there are wounds on the body or an infirmity in some limb; premature death of mother.

MOON AND MERCURY: Infirmity in some limb; is wise, well read, and learned; profuse in speech; a person of a high order.

MOON AND JUPITER: Very lucky; endowed with wealth and prosperity; persevering and possessed of all kinds of comforts and happiness.

MOON AND VENUS: May have a stepmother; his wife may not be free from blemish or he may have a liaison with a profligate; prosperous but under the influence of his inferiors; his health is not good.

MOON AND SATURN: Sinful acts; he tears asunder the religious precepts; the mother is fallen in respect to social standards.

MARS AND MERCURY: Handsome appearance; clever in interpretation of learned treatises; enjoys luxuries but is always restless and agitated.

MARS AND JUPITER: Much respected; endowed with plenty of wealth; a hard person to deal with; suffers from some chronic ailment; wounds and scars.

MARS AND VENUS: Lives abroad; cruel and quarrelsome; often resorts to lying and deception; ungrateful; frustrated with women.

MARS AND SATURN: Sinful; dirty conduct; attached to others' wives; devoid of wealth and happiness; has no relations or friends whom he may call his own.

MERCURY AND JUPITER: Wise and well-versed in learned treatises; wealthy and prosperous; a connoisseur of arts and crafts; occupies a high and powerful position; speaks endearingly.

MERCURY AND VENUS: Handsome appearance; eloquent and persuasive speech; learned and well-renowned; persevering; inclined to settle matters with tact and diplomacy.

MERCURY AND SATURN: Clever and capable; wealthy but suffers in respect to health; has a good circle of friends; very garrulous; on inimical terms with ethics.

JUPITER AND VENUS: Long-lived; endowed with wealth and many comforts and luxuries; his speech is good; he occupies a lofty position like that of a king.

JUPITER AND SATURN: Much respected but suffers in health; has no relations or friends whom he may call his own or else lives separately from them; has wealth and jewelry.

VENUS AND SATURN: Has wealth and sons; is well-bred and courteous; earns name and fame; is a favorite of the king, but suffers from ill health.

All these effects have to be appraised in light of the sign occupying the Ninth house, the lordship of the planets involved, and any aspect or aspects the conjunction may be receiving. Benefic aspects mitigate the evil and enhance the good. Malefic aspects enhance the evil and mitigate the good.

CONJUNCTIONS OF THREE PLANETS

SUN, MOON AND MARS: Dry in body, speech or manners; marks from wounds; devoid of father or mother or else prematurely separated from them; inimical and hurtful; occupies a low position early in life.

SUN, MOON AND MERCURY: Valorous and truthful; inimical to all; suffers much distress; is androgynous in appearance.

SUN, MOON AND JUPITER: A first class gentleman, endowed with wealth, comforts, vehicles and happiness.

SUN, MOON AND VENUS: Agreeable in speech; diplomatic; favored by the king, but all his wealth and happiness are destroyed due to quarrels with women or because of a quarrelsome wife.

SUN, MOON AND SATURN: Unpopular and inimical to people; very strong and aggressive, a bully in speech and conduct; serves others.

SUN, MARS AND MERCURY: Agreeable speech; lives primarily abroad (or far from his birthplace); intent on combat; cruel; very angry, and revengeful like a snake.

SUN, MARS AND JUPITER: Industrious and actively engaged in work; endowed with many qualities of heart and mind; devoted to gods and manes;[1] has a wealthy wife.

SUN, MARS AND VENUS: Comes from a good family but is quarrelsome; very active; inimical to many; seduces unmarried girls.

---

1   The word manes designates various spiritual entities above the purely human level, but less exalted than the gods.

SUN, MARS AND SATURN: Bold and courageous; of low position or conduct; cruel; given to lying and deception; unpopular; separated from the father at an early age.

SUN, MERCURY AND JUPITER: Handsome appearance; dresses well; is patiently persevering; wealthy and very lucky; a favorite of the king.

SUN, MERCURY AND VENUS: Lustrous and handsome; has much stamina; overcomes enemies and opposition; occupies a high position, equivalent to that of a monarch.

SUN, MERCURY AND SATURN: Very impudent but clever and capable; lives away from home; attached to others' wives; sinful; false in speech and conduct; irreligious.

SUN, JUPITER AND VENUS: Attractive and handsome, with a good memory; intelligent, learned and wise; has mastery over several aspects of life.

SUN, JUPITER AND SATURN: Has much virility and prowess; has many good qualities; wealthy; lords it over people like a monarch.

SUN, VENUS AND SATURN: Uncouth appearance, having no luster; devoid of wealth; punished by the government; foolish in speech and/or conduct.

MOON, MARS AND MERCURY: Suffers much distress in the early part of life due to destruction of everything, but later becomes rich and is possessed of gold and jewels.

MOON, MARS AND JUPITER: Handsome, wise, learned and wealthy; has control over his senses (i.e. he is not led away by unworthy temptations); devoted to the gods and to religious preceptors.

MOON, MARS AND VENUS: Unattractive, with wounds or marks on the body; inclined towards homosexuality; fond of women and under their influence; wastes health and wealth on women.

MOON, MARS AND SATURN: Unlucky and low in conduct or position; uncared for or forsaken by the mother in childhood; his mother's family falls into misfortune.

MOON, MERCURY AND JUPITER: There is increase in the dynasty (i.e. sons and grandsons are born); the native occupies a kingly position; he administrates some educational or religious institution; has many friends, as well as means and expedients for accomplishment.

MOON, MERCURY AND VENUS: Cheerful disposition; prizes self-respect; has a large circle of friends; likely to have a stepmother; inclined to settle controversial points by cool persuasion.

MOON, MERCURY AND SATURN: Uncouth appearance; evil intentions; cruel conduct; leads a humble life; strong but avoids the arena of battle.

MOON, JUPITER AND VENUS: Occupies a lofty position equal to that of a king; according to classical texts, if he is born in a royal family he verily becomes a king.

MOON, JUPITER AND SATURN: Well-bred and courteous; of endearing speech; well-versed in learned treatises; famous; wedded to truth.

MOON, VENUS AND SATURN: Gains from agriculture; attached to women and their maintenance; not free from religious blemish; well renowned and glorified.

MARS, MERCURY AND JUPITER: Brilliantly courageous; optimistic; learned; fulfills his promises; a person of a high order; occupies a lofty position.

MARS, MERCURY AND VENUS: Has mastery over several branches of learning; well-renowned; is truthful to gentlefolk but has a fiery temper.

MARS, MERCURY AND SATURN: Clever in deceiving others; has lower mental and emotional qualities such as hatred, malice, or anger; not learned; does not grasp the reasoning put forward by others.

MARS, JUPITER AND VENUS: Much respected and wealthy but resorts to low practices in dealing with others; meets disappointment in love affairs; has unreliable associates; his health is not very good.

MARS, JUPITER AND SATURN: His conduct is not above board; hypocritical in religion; earns wealth but dissipates it; cannot depend on his friends; his health suffers.

MARS, VENUS AND SATURN: Sharp practices in business; very lusty and hankering for satisfaction; receives patronage from influential people and earns money, but remains discontented.

MERCURY, JUPITER AND VENUS: Highly religious and learned; well renowned; calm and free from anxiety; according to classical texts, "pure like a god;" a ruler of men.

MERCURY, JUPITER AND SATURN: Wise and learned, wealthy and prosperous; suffers in health; cannot rely on his friends and relations.

MERCURY, VENUS AND SATURN: Very good memory; learned; very cultured and endearing in speech; comes into prominence; enjoys the comforts of life.

JUPITER, VENUS AND SATURN: Handsome and attractive appearance; happy and comfortable life, having plenty of food, drink and luxury items.

For four or more planets, the reader may return to Chapter III and adjust the interpretations more specifically to the Ninth house. It should be kept in mind that a cluster of planets in the Ninth house is always good, if Jupiter or Mercury is one of them — or, better still, if *both* Mercury and Jupiter are there along with other planets. Devoid of Mercury and Jupiter, such a configuration is seldom good. Why? Because most of the remaining planets are malefics, and the general principle is that malefics spoil the house they tenant, the exception being a malefic in its own sign. (Mars and Saturn in Capricorn in the Ninth, for instance, would not be evil because Mars would be exalted therein and Saturn in his own house.)

JUPITER IN THE NINTH

The old masters have given in detail the effects of Jupiter in the Ninth house and according to his aspects from other planets.

Jupiter in the Ninth house and aspected by:

SUN: Equal to a king.

MOON: Handsome appearance; much enjoyment of all kinds.

MARS: Rich and lustrous.

MERCURY: Rich.

VENUS: Possesses cattle, wealth and vehicles.

SATURN: Possesses immovable properties (i.e. real estate), also buffaloes and donkeys.

SUN AND MOON: Very prosperous and beloved of his parents; well-renowned, having several wives; equal to a king.

SUN AND MARS: Possesses vehicles and a large family (in ancient India, there was an extended family system; hence a "large family" does not simply mean many children).

SUN AND MERCURY: Soft, handsome and attractive body; wise, having health, jewelry and an excellent relationship with damsels or one's wife; well versed in poetry and the arts.

SUN AND VENUS: Well-mannered and fond of social gatherings and celebrations; possessing goats, cows, buffaloes and elephants (these indicators of wealth in ancient times must of course be re-interpreted in terms of modern urban populations).

SUN AND SATURN: Wise, virtuous, having many good qualities; well-renowned; hoards his money; intent on collecting money and commodities; a leader of men or the chief man of the region.

MOON AND MARS: Handsome; prosperous; commander of an army or minister to a king; has all kinds of comforts and conveniences.

MOON AND MERCURY: Very intelligent and discreet; of a forgiving disposition; enjoys fine houses and "the pleasures of the bed"; a very comfortable life.

MOON AND VENUS: Always intent on engaging in work (i.e. a man of action); bold and chivalrous; very wealthy; enjoys others' wives; does not have a son.

MOON AND SATURN: Very proud or intoxicated; has a long and stable life; often lives abroad or far from his native place; lacking in noble qualities; resorts to lies; enters into disputes and controversies.

MARS AND MERCURY: Very courteous and wise; has many admirable qualities; learned; accepts good advice; dresses very attractively.

MARS AND VENUS: Has many good qualities but is cruel; very clever and capable; lives abroad; learned and wealthy.

MARS AND SATURN: Of low caliber or conduct; a back-biter; lives abroad; on inimical terms with others; keeps company with unstable persons.

MERCURY AND VENUS: Attractive personality; cool-tempered and courteous; appreciates and accepts advice; learned; a connoisseur of crafts; foppishly dressed.

MERCURY AND SATURN: Handsome and comely, eloquent and learned, chivalrous and courteous; leads a happy and comfortable life.

VENUS AND SATURN: Head of a town; wealthy and prosperous; occupies a high political or administrative position.

Readers will note that when two planets aspect Jupiter in the Ninth, they need not necessarily be in the Third house nor need they be conjoined. For example, Mars in the Second or Sixth from the Ascendant will have a full aspect on the Ninth as will Saturn in the Seventh or Twelfth. The resulting situation should be interpreted according to the guidelines given under Mars and Saturn aspecting Jupiter in the Ninth.

The effects of one planet aspecting Jupiter in the Ninth apply in greater measure if the aspecting planet happens to be the dispositor of Jupiter (i.e. lord of the sign tenanted by Jupiter). If all six planets aspect Jupiter in the Ninth, the native will be very brilliant, extremely wealthy and virtuous, and will occupy a kingly position. Strong benefics in the Ninth confer kingdom (according to the ancient texts), immovable properties, wealth, granaries (one of the chief assets in ancient times) and long life. Malefic planets in their enemies' signs or in debilitation in the Ninth, unless aspected by benefics, make one weak, poor, and uncouth, leading an obscure life. But even malefics, if in their own sign in the Ninth, are auspicious and show very good effects, particularly if aspected by a benefic.

All planets, if in their sign of exaltation in the Ninth, raise a person to a lofty position and confer upon him gold and riches, and if the exalted planet is aspected by a benefic the native overcomes all obstacles and opposition and gains wide fame.

8

THE
MOON-SIGN

In the Western system the sun-sign occupies pride of place, and the astrological literature abounds in books and booklets giving predictions on the basis of the natal location of the Sun. In Hindu astrology the location and position of the Sun, as well as its conjunctions and aspects, are important factors; but the Sun is not accorded the same importance as it is in the West. Instead, the moon-sign (i.e. the sidereal sign in which the Moon is located at birth) is the most important single factor. In northern and northwestern India, the moon-sign chart is included along with the birth chart, even in the most basic horoscopes. What is the moon-sign chart? Instead of the rising sign or Ascendant being placed at top center in the figure, as it usually is in those parts of India, the moon-sign is placed there, as if it were the Ascendant or First house. The other planets are then placed in the houses corresponding to their natal sign positions. Thus we may mark in which house each planet is posited as computed from the natal Moon. A chart is traditionally judged from the point of view of this Lunar Ascendant (Chandra Lagna, from Chandra=Moon and Lagna=Ascendant) as well as from the actual Ascendant.

Rudra Bhatta, on page 23 of his *Vivarana*, states:

> In a nativity, fifty percent of the effects should be ascribed to the rising sign and the other fifty percent as computed from the moon-sign.

There are two relevant traditions, dating from time immemorial. The first is that between the Ascendant and the Moon, more importance should be attached to whichever is stronger; i.e. if the Moon is stronger, treat it as the Ascendant and see how the planets are disposed from the moon-sign. The second tradition is that the effects of planets as disposed from the moon-sign are felt in greater measure after the age of thirty-two. We have found authority in classical texts for the first premise, and the second is based on tradition. Many astrological works note special configurations as producing particular effects when the planetary positions are counted from the rising sign, and then add that these should be computed from the moon-sign also. Mantreshwar, for example, describes certain effects for the rising sign and then adds that these should be applied to the moon-sign also.[1] Just as the five planets (i.e. except for the Sun and Moon, which are technically luminaries rather than planets) in their own signs or signs of exaltation are deemed highly beneficent, conferring wealth and position if posited in one of the angles (the First, Fourth, Seventh or Tenth house from the Ascendant), in a similar manner they are deemed to confer the same excellent results if, instead of being in an angle from the Ascendant, they are in an angle from the moon-sign.[2]

Texts have laid down the results of planetary conjunctions as counted from the moon-sign, and all the conjunctions delineated in this chapter are to be considered in this light. When we say "in the Second house," it refers to the second from the Moon; when we say "in the Tenth," it means the tenth from the Moon.

A conjunction of two or more benefic planets is good in the Second or Twelfth. A conjunction of two benefics in one of those houses with a single benefic in the other lends support to the conjunction. Of course, if two benefics conjoin in the Second, it is better than their conjunction in the Twelfth.

But according to one school *any* conjunction, whether of benefics or of malefics, in either of these two houses causes wealth and luxurious living. According to this school, even Mars or Saturn in the Second or Twelfth is not wholly evil but gives mixed results. We, however, do not favor Mars or Saturn in either the Second or Twelfth except when in their own houses or exalted in the Second. One important consideration is that although the position of a planet from the Moon is one factor, the planet's position from the Ascendant also remains vital. An inference must therefore be drawn by assessing its position from both starting points. For example, suppose Pisces is rising and the Moon is in Sagittarius in the Tenth. If Mars is in Scorpio, in the Twelfth from the Moon, he will be the lord of the Ninth in the Ninth from the Ascendant. Mars is a natural malefic, but in his own sign in the Ninth house from the rising sign, he enjoys first class placement. Or take another example. Suppose Libra is the rising sign, the Moon is in Aquarius, and Saturn, lord of the Fourth and Fifth, is in Capricorn. In such a case Saturn in the Twelfth from the natal Moon will not be evil. Rather, he will be good. Thus various factors have to be synthesized and the ultimate inference drawn only after blending the results from more points of view than one.

---

1   *Phala Deepika,* Chapter 9, verse 13.
2   *Ibid.,* Chapter 6, verse 4.

Besides, for fuller assessment, the sign in which the planets are conjoined also has a say. For example, if the Moon is in Aquarius and Jupiter and Venus are in Pisces, then Jupiter will be in his own sign and Venus exalted. Also, as counted from Aquarius (the moon-sign), Jupiter will be the lord of the Second and Eleventh and Venus of the Fourth and Ninth houses. Thus it will be a conjunction not only of two benefics in a sign favorable to both, but also of the lords of the Second, Fourth, Ninth and Eleventh. These shades of influence due to sign and lordship must always be kept in mind.

A conjunction of Mercury, Jupiter and Venus in the Third, Sixth, Tenth or Eleventh is extremely good for finances. Suppose two of these benefics conjoin in any of the above houses and the third planet is also in one of the above houses though not conjoined. This is good, but a conjunction of all three in any of the above houses is better.

Similarly, if there is a conjunction of Mercury, Jupiter and Venus in the Sixth, Seventh or Eighth, it is an excellent configuration for wealth, position and longevity. Even if there is a conjunction of two of these benefics in one of the above houses, say the Seventh, and the third is in the Sixth or Eighth, or if the conjunction is in the Sixth and the other is in the Seventh or Eighth, or the conjunction is in the Eighth and the other is in the Sixth or Seventh, it is extremely good.

Any conjunction — whether of benefics, malefics, or a mixture of both — in the Eleventh from the Moon brings in much money. A subtle distinction, however, is that benefics bring money by ethical means which are above board while malefics make one earn a livelihood by methods involving hardship to others and which may also be underhanded.

It is good to have a conjunction of malefics in the Third or Sixth from the Moon. Such a conjunction increases the power and prowess of the native, but a conjunction of malefics is most inauspicious if in the moon-sign itself or in the Eighth or Twelfth house from it.

If the Moon is not conjoined with any planet, and if there is no planet in the Second or Twelfth from the Moon, it is good to have a conjunction (or even a single planet) in the Fourth, Seventh or Tenth from the Moon. Without such a configuration the native remains poor. Of course, it is best to have Jupiter, or even Venus or Mercury in an angle. But it is better to have a conjunction of malefics or even a single malefic in an angle from the Moon rather than no planet at all. But the presence of a malefic here is only favorable as a contingency when there is no planet in the Second or Twelfth from the Moon. For these yogas (configurations), the Nodes of the Moon, Rahu and Ketu, are not taken into account.

In judging the quality of the Moon, a few criteria have been laid down. First, a waxing Moon is good, while a waning Moon is not. Second, on the fourteenth and fifteenth day of the dark fortnight the Moon is extremely feeble and therefore not good at all. If the Moon has only five digits or less in strength, he is weak; from five to ten digits, of middling strength, and with more than ten digits, strong. Another classification rests on the basis of whether the birth is during the dark or bright fortnight, during day or night, and whether the Moon is above the horizon (in the visible half of the zodiac) or below (in the invisible half). The judgment in regard to these factors is as follows:

First, if the birth is during the day (from sunrise to sunset is deemed day and from sunset to sunrise night) and the Moon is located in the visible half of the zodiac, he is deemed inauspicious. Second, the Moon in the dark fortnight with little digital strength is deemed weak (and therefore evil).

Thus if the birth occurs during the dark fortnight (waning Moon), if the Moon has only a few digits in strength, and if it is a diurnal[3] chart with the Moon located in the visible half of the zodiac, it will be extremely weak and inauspicious — and how much good can any planet do for it, no matter how well placed? But in a nocturnal chart, if the birth is in the bright fortnight (waxing Moon) and the Moon has good digital strength and lies in the visible half of the zodiac, it will be extremely auspicious and planets well placed from it will show excellent results.

Thus in the dark fortnight the Moon below the horizon will be auspicious in a diurnal chart but inauspicious in a nocturnal chart; in the bright fortnight, in a diurnal chart, he will not be unfavorable even when above the horizon and in a nocturnal chart he is fairly good even in the invisible half.

The Tenth house governs many affairs, chief of which are action, good and bad deeds, vocation or profession, efforts for earning, rank and status, power, position and one's standing in society, and the authority one exercises over people. As will be readily observed, all these are inter-connected — corollaries flowing from the main proposition.

In view of the moon-sign occupying the same importance as the rising sign, the older masters have described in detail the effects of conjunctions of two or more planets in the Tenth from the Moon and the same are succinctly stated below.

---

3   Birth charts of persons born during the day are called diurnal charts;
     those of persons born at night are called nocturnal charts.

But before we do this, it is necessary to add that one of the cardinal principles of Hindu astrology is that a person puts forth efforts to earn according to (1) the planet in the Tenth from the Ascendant and/or the Sun and/or Moon, (2) the navamsha dispositor of the lord of the Tenth from the Ascendant and/or the Sun and/or Moon.

Each planet, regardless of its house lordship, signifies certain matters and affairs, and of these he is called a significator (karaka in Sanskrit). Let us succinctly state what each planet signifies:

Sun	Father, the classes or castes (as distinct from the masses), gold, people in authority, government
Moon	Mother, ladies, liquids, silver, masses, white things
Mars	Brothers, enemies, copper, fire, immovable properties (real estate), daring and courage, red things, the military, police, arms and ammunition
Mercury	Speech, reading, writing, transmission, friends, the press, publicity, a link between two parties, green things
Jupiter	Sons, brothers, religious preceptors, wealthy persons, banking, gold, treasury, teaching, law, yellow things; and, in a female nativity, the husband
Venus	The wife (in a man's chart), sex (also in male charts), fashionable articles, jewelry, entertainment, cooperation, edibles and drinks, white commodities
Saturn	Authority, labor, servants, iron, oil, minerals, agriculture, black things, hard work, underhanded means, low people

There is gain of money from the indicated sources according to which planet or planets are in the Tenth or Eleventh from the Moon. Similarly, the Tenth and Eleventh houses from the Ascendant and the Sun must be examined.

In earlier chapters, we have delineated the effects of a conjunction of two planets in the Tenth house from the Ascendant. However, we have not given the individual effects of planets by sign or house. Such a study would require too much space, and since we have already dealt with the matter exhaustively in our other book, *Hindu Predictive Astrology,* we do not wish to repeat what we have stated elsewhere. But the earlier book did not delineate the effects of single planets occupying the Tenth from the Moon. In order to understand and better appreciate the effects of conjunctions of planets in the Tenth from the Moon, we shall first state the basic effects of each planet there.

SINGLE PLANETS IN THE TENTH FROM THE MOON

SUN: Healthy, much stamina, successful in undertakings and enterprises; wealthy and prosperous, exalted position, extends protection and patronage to a large number of people.

MARS: Bold and daring, cruel, devoted to sports but sometimes intent upon afflicting people; is generally in the company of rough and unrefined people, always hankering after the desires of the flesh.

MERCURY: Wise and intelligent, well read and learned, clever in arts and crafts; rich and renowned, one of the king's leading men.

JUPITER: Religious, successful in accumulating wealth, prosperous; of noble and praiseworthy conduct and famous, a minister to the king.

VENUS: Handsome, soft and attractive body, rich and wealthy; accomplishes whatever he undertakes, much respected by the king.

SATURN: Suffers from chronic disease, always restless and agitated in work; poor and miserable, suffers in respect to children (i.e. no children or no happiness from them).

TWO PLANETS IN THE TENTH FROM THE MOON

SUN AND MARS: Engaged in much active work but suffers from respiratory or wasting diseases; may excel in astrology and logic; excessive cupidity; one's profession is connected with fire (i.e. factories) or with the bearing of arms.

SUN AND MERCURY: Gains from trade and commerce; enjoys apparel and jewelry; may earn his livelihood in a profession connected with water (i.e. irrigation, dams, hydro-electric engineering, shipping, import-export, etc.).

SUN AND JUPITER: Successful in enterprises undertaken; much respected by the government; chivalrous, persevering and renowned.

SUN AND VENUS: Handsome; extends patronage to his own people or is patronized by them; accumulates wealth due to receiving help, assistance and patronage from women; a favorite of the king.

SUN AND SATURN: Follows a humble profession of service; may suffer some kind of punishment; suffers from theft, or his property is misappropriated by others; miserable, miserly and humiliated.

MARS AND MERCURY: Has a strong opposition or a large number of enemies; clever, bold and very chivalrous; has a good knowledge of weapons or machinery; is long-lived.

MARS AND JUPITER: A leader of men or armies; gains from or through the agency of friends; progressive life and living due to helpers and associates.

MARS AND VENUS: Lives abroad; income from trade and commerce, from gold and pearls (i.e. jewelry, articles of fashion and luxury), and also due to the favor and patronage of ladies.

MARS AND SATURN: Daring and courageous; actively engaged in work, but mean; likely to suffer from some chronic health complaint.

MERCURY AND JUPITER: Wealthy; respected by kings; religious; a leader of groups of people; well-renowned.

MERCURY AND VENUS: Has many hearty friends; happy and learned; enjoys his wife or women generally; much pleasure; minister to a king.

MERCURY AND SATURN: A maker of pottery or other articles made from material taken out of the earth; well read in many branches of learning; good in calligraphy or as an artist or author; well-renowned.

JUPITER AND VENUS: Occupies a high position in the government; very learned and capable; very optimistic; a leader of Brahmins (the priestly class among Hindus, or, in a more modern context, scholars).

JUPITER AND SATURN: Low in conduct; afflicts some but obliges others; acts soberly and engages in large-scale work; occupies a permanent posiion; commences work in a steady manner.

VENUS AND SATURN: An artist or a physician; deals in dyes and powders (i.e. powdered material); may gain much money through scents, perfumeries or aromatic articles.

THREE PLANETS IN THE TENTH FROM MOON

SUN, MARS AND MERCURY: Much praised; a person of a very high order (i.e. of noble conduct and sterling merits); respected by all; equal to a king.

SUN, MARS AND JUPITER: Handsome appearance; wealthy and prosperous; crushes his enemies and opposition.

SUN, MARS AND VENUS: Daring and courageous but cruel; very clever and crafty in appropriating others' wealth.

SUN, MARS AND SATURN: Engaged in cruelty and afflicting others; not discreet; sinful and of evil conduct.

SUN, MERCURY AND JUPITER: A very handsome and admirable person; learned, loving and helpful to his relations; highly religious and benevolent.

SUN, MERCURY AND VENUS: Cool-tempered but un-vanquished by others; religious, having a good name and wide fame; very lucky and possessed of numerous luxury items.

SUN, MERCURY AND SATURN: Very active and not of stable disposition; his body may be hurt by fire or a weapon; cruel, ill-tempered and unmannerly.

SUN, JUPITER AND VENUS: Lovable personality; earns money by brains and learning; given to religious practices; always enjoying the fruits of his prosperity (i.e. leading a life of comfort and luxury).

SUN, JUPITER AND SATURN: Though his conduct is not in accordance with moral or religious codes, yet he is much honored by the people; very persevering.

SUN, VENUS AND SATURN: Very avaricious, intent upon appropriating wealth; active but not steady in resolution; alienates the sympathy of all.

MARS, MERCURY AND JUPITER: Religious, with a large family (not necessarily many children, since extended families were formerly prevalent in India); is learned and wealthy.

MARS, MERCURY AND VENUS: Very much adored by the people; engaged in artistic work and the production or trade of articles of embellishment and beauty (e.g. scents, flowers, silk, dresses, jewelry, cosmetics).

MARS, MERCURY AND SATURN: Of uncouth appearance as regards either person or dress; indolent and given to much sleeping; not religious, wicked.

MARS, JUPITER AND VENUS: Brave and valorous; wealthy; pays homage to gods and Brahmins (i.e. is religious and charitable).

MARS, JUPITER AND SATURN: Devoid of learning and wealth; not much assertiveness or courage; suffers from some infirmity in a limb or is restless and agitated; is low in conduct and/or position, neither comfortable nor happy.

MARS, VENUS AND SATURN: A person of a high order in qualities or position; wealthy and religious, engaged in many pursuits; inclined to live in country houses or forests; a minister to a king or of some equivalent status.

MERCURY, JUPITER AND VENUS: If the conjunction is in Taurus or Libra it generates various kinds of good influence (e.g. health, wealth, learning, high status), but if it takes place in any other sign the native suffers in health and is sickly.

MERCURY, JUPITER AND SATURN: Comely appearance, fond of traveling, engaged in writing prose or poetry or working as an artist; very wealthy, with many good servants.

MERCURY, VENUS AND SATURN: Given to the study of sciences or else a wrestler; always actively engaged in work; exercises self-restraint and lives abroad.

JUPITER, VENUS AND SATURN: Religious, learned and merciful.

FOUR PLANETS IN THE TENTH FROM THE MOON

SUN, MARS, MERCURY AND JUPITER: Engaged in various pursuits; daring and courageous, with scars on the body due to hurts or diseases; generous.

SUN, MARS, MERCURY AND VENUS: Proficient in manufacturing or trading articles of fashion and enjoyment which afford pleasure to the senses; may be a writer, painter, artist or sculptor.

SUN, MARS, MERCURY AND SATURN: Possesses wealth, conveyances and elephants (indicators of aristocracy in former times).

SUN, MERCURY, JUPITER AND VENUS: Mild and good-natured, though he may come from a lower-class family; of noble conduct; engaged in work connected with land and agriculture.

SUN, MERCURY, JUPITER AND SATURN: Cruel, hypocritical, and fraudulent; intent upon and engaged in cheating (whether he will be a small vendor with false weights and measures or a multi-millionaire rogue raiding major corporations will depend on other factors).

SUN, MERCURY, VENUS AND SATURN: Handsome but hard-hearted; eloquent; engaged in agriculture, excavation, minerals etc.

SUN, JUPITER, VENUS AND SATURN: Engaged in many pursuits or a variety of work; lives in a place other than his homeland.

MARS, MERCURY, JUPITER AND VENUS: Clever and capable, very courageous, never vanquished in battle (i.e. he is not crushed by his competitors; rather, he annihilates them).

MARS, MERCURY, JUPITER AND SATURN: Uncouth in person or dress; always intent upon work; annihilates all his enemies on the battlefield.

MARS, MERCURY, VENUS AND SATURN: Large body, very learned; bold and a good fighter.

MARS, JUPITER, VENUS AND SATURN: Very persevering, not easily ruffled; has a large family and much wealth; may have a number of people serving under him.

MERCURY, JUPITER, VENUS AND SATURN: Patient, peaceful mind, unruffled by emotions; very intelligent and possessed of a good memory, popular and much adored by the people.

The good effects described above manifest fully if the conjunction is not aspected by one or more malefics, and the evil effects are mitigated if the cluster of planets is aspected by a benefic or benefics. This is a general principle, applicable to everything in this book.

9
IMPORTANT
COMBINATIONS

In earlier chapters we covered the conjunctions and aspects of the planets. We have noted that the lordships of the houses should always be taken into account, and we have provided guidelines to help in judgment. But anyone who reads this book will naturally be interested in the yogas (special configurations or combinations arising out of conjunctions and aspects) which have a bearing on particular affairs. We detail some of them in this chapter. We have not arranged them in terms of planets or the lords of the houses but have grouped them according to the points under inquiry. Some preliminary notes, however, have been added for better understanding and appreciation.

HEALTH AND DISEASES

The human body has been allocated to the twelve signs and the twelve houses, with some overlapping jurisdictions which we shall presently explain. But before we do so we shall state how the human body has been divided into twelve sectors:

1. Head
2. Eyes, face, and the upper part of the throat
3. Lower part of throat, the ears, shoulders, arms, & hands
4. Chest and heart
5. Stomach
6. Waist (upper half)
7. Waist (lower half)
8. Genitals and organs of excretion
9. Thighs and hips
10. Knees and back
11. Calves of the legs
12. Feet

This allocation differs in some respects from those given in Western astrological texts. But we are concerned here with Hindu astrology.

These sectors have been assigned to the twelve signs in regular order from (1) Aries to (12) Pisces. Thus if there is a malefic aspected by another malefic or a conjunction of malefics in any sign, the corresponding part of the body suffers. Conversely, if there is a conjunction of benefics or a benefic aspected by another benefic, that part of the body is strong, healthy and attractive.

We have stated above that the jurisdiction of the signs and houses are overlapping. What do we mean by this? We mean that the signs do not have *exclusive* jurisdiction, for these twelve sectors of the human body are allocated to the twelve houses as well, in regular order from (1) the First house to (12) the Twelfth. Hence a conjunction of malefics in the Second or a malefic in the Second aspected by another malefic will damage the part of the body governed by that house, while benefics do the opposite. But there are exceptions. Venus and the Moon are both benefics, but their conjunction in the Second or the presence of one in the Second aspected by the other from a different house will damage the eyesight. Another peculiarity is: from the cusp or ascending degree of the First house to the cusp of the Seventh (i.e. the invisible half of the zodiac) governs the right side of the body, while the other area from the cusp of the Seventh to the cusp of the First (the visible half of the zodiac) governs the left side — thus the Second house is the right eye, the Twelfth house the left eye, the Third house the right ear, the Eleventh house the left ear and so on.

Hindu astrologers have gone very deeply into the matter, as the following dictum will show. Generally the child is born head first; that is the normal course of delivery. But, according to an old master, if the child is born feet first the First house denotes the feet, the Second the calves of the leg, the Third the knees and so on, in the reverse order.

1. The lord of the First is in an angle, a trine or in the Eleventh, well placed by sign or navamsha (i.e. in its own navamsha) and conjoined with or aspected by a benefic and not conjoined with or aspected by a malefic: Healthy, long-lived and prosperous.

2. The Moon is strong in digital strength, well-placed and conjoined with or aspected by benefics: Healthy and long-lived.

3. A conjunction of benefics in the First house: Good for health.

4. All the angles occupied by benefics with mutual aspects from both the First and Seventh and the Fourth and Tenth: Good for health and prosperity. A benefic in the First aspected by another benefic from the Seventh is good in its own right.

5. Malefics instead of benefics in the First house: Ill health and diseases. But a malefic in its own house or exalted is not bad.

6. Malefics (including Rahu and Ketu) instead of benefics in the angles: Unhealthy, vicious and unlucky. But if the malefics are in their own signs or in exaltation they prove good.

7. The First house untenanted and aspected by his own lord or by benefics: Good health.

8. The First house untenanted but aspected by a malefic (unless the malefic concerned is the lord of the First): Unfavorable for health.

9. The Sun in the First house in Aquarius causes heart trouble, particularly so if aspected by a malefic.

10. The lord of the Sixth or a planet occupying or aspecting the Sixth, weak and conjoined with or aspected by a malefic: Ill health.

11. The lord of the Sixth is a benefic in an angle or trine, conjoined with or aspected by a benefic: Freedom from disease.

12. A malefic in the Ascendant conjoined with an enemy: Wounds on the body or poor health.

13. The lord of the Sixth, if malefic, in the First or Eighth house aspected by another malefic: Wounds or disease.

14. The lord of the Ascendant in the Sixth, Eighth or Twelfth conjoined with a malefic or aspected by a malefic: Sickly and obscure life.

15. The lord of the Sixth in the First conjoined with Rahu or Ketu: A wound in the body.

16. The Sun and Moon conjunct in Cancer or Leo leads to emaciation or some chronic wasting disease.

17. If the lord of the Second and Rahu conjoin with the lord of the Third there is throat disease.

18. Mars and Saturn together in the Second house cause diseases.

19. If Rahu is in the First house and conjunct the lords of the First and Third: Danger from snakes.

20. Mars conjoined with a strong Saturn in the Third: Skin diseases.

21. The lord of the Third conjoined with Mercury, both aspected by a malefic: Throat trouble.

22. The Moon, Venus and the lord of the Second conjoined together: Damage to eyesight.

23. The Sun, Venus and the lord of the First conjoined in the invisible half of the zodiac: Deteriorating vision. (The half of the zodiac from the cusp of the First house to the cusp of the Seventh is invisible. The other half is the visible part.)

24. The lords of the First, Second, Seventh and Twelfth conjoined in the Sixth, Eighth or Twelfth from the Ascendant: Loss of vision.

25. Venus conjunct with the lord of the Fifth and Sixth houses in the First house: Loss of vision.

26. The lord of the Third and Mars conjoined in the First: Diseases of the ear.

27. The Moon in the Twelfth aspected by the Sun in the Sixth or vice versa: Eye trouble for the native and for his wife.

28. Of the five planets Sun, Moon, Mars, Venus and Saturn: Any two or more conjoined in the Second, Sixth, Eighth or Twelfth damages the eyesight.

29. The Moon, applying to the Sun and within 24 degrees from him, conjoined with Saturn in the Twelfth from the Ascendant: Schizophrenia, brain trouble.

30. A conjunction of malefics in the Third, Fifth, Ninth or Eleventh, unaspected by any benefic, causes ear trouble or deafness.

31. A malefic in the Third or Eleventh aspected by another malefic will cause the same effect as above.

32. Jupiter in the Ascendant aspected by Saturn in the Seventh: Diseases arising from an imbalance of vata. (For example, gout, rheumatism, etc.)

33. Jupiter in the Ascendant aspected by Mars in the Seventh: Mental diseases.

34. If Aries, Taurus or Sagittarius is rising and aspected by malefics, the native has very ugly or crooked teeth.

35. If Aries, Taurus, Leo, Scorpio, Sagittarius, Capricorn or Aquarius is rising and the Sun is in the First house aspected by a malefic: The native is bald.

36. The Sun in the Fifth or Ninth aspected by a malefic: The eyesight suffers.

37. Mars or Saturn in the Fifth or Ninth, not conjoined with or aspected by a benefic: Diseases, particularly if the malefic in the Fifth or Ninth is aspected by another malefic.

38. The Sun in the Tenth aspecting Mars in the Fourth: Hurt by a stone or a fall from a hill.

39. The Sun and Moon together in Pisces in the Ascendant: Danger of drowning.

40. Saturn in Cancer aspected by the Moon in Capricorn: Asceticism.

41. Sun or Mars in the Fourth aspected by Saturn in the Tenth: Hurt from weapons.

42. The Sun and Moon conjoined in the Fourth aspecting Mars in the Tenth: Wounds from weapons.

43. The Sun in the Fourth aspected by Mars in the Tenth and Mars aspected by Saturn: Serious hurt by a wooden log or a stick of bamboo (i.e. a lathi), etc.

44. The Sun in the Tenth aspected by Mars in the Fourth: A fall from a vehicle.

45. Malefics conjoined in the Seventh: Unsymmetrical or crooked teeth or dental ailments in general.

46. The Moon in the Second or Eighth: Much perspiration. If the Moon is conjoined with or aspected by a malefic, the odor will be particularly obnoxious.

47. Mars and Mercury conjoined in the Tenth: The body has a bad odor.

48. A conjunction of malefics in the Eighth: Many diseases.

49. Mars and Ketu in the Fourth: A fall from a vehicle or while mounting steps.

LONGEVITY

There are elaborate rules for determining longevity. Some of them involve intricate calculations, but some general rules can be given simply on the basis of conjunctions and aspects. The rules given for judging good health apply to longevity also. According to Hindu astrology, these rules should be applied to the charts of adults and not to those of children, because when, in the birth chart of parents or of either parent, there are malefic configurations for the death of children, then their children do not survive. Before we detail the rules below, we would like to define for our readers the words "short," "medium," and "long" life as used in the context of Hindu astrology. They have acquired a technical meaning: Up to the age of 32 means a short life, from 32 to 64 medium, and beyond 64 long. Others define the short span up to 36 years, medium up to 72, and long beyond that.

1. The lord of the Eighth in the Sixth or Twelfth conjoined with a malefic: The native's life span will be short if the lord of the First is weak.

2. The lord of the Eighth in the Eighth aspected by a benefic: Long-lived.

3. The lords of the First and Eighth together in the Sixth or Twelfth from the Ascendant and aspected by a benefic: Long-lived.

4. The lords of the First, Eighth and Tenth in an angle or trine or in the Eleventh (severally or jointly) and aspected by a benefic or benefics: Long life. But if these lords are weak and conjoined with Saturn it signifies a short life.

5. The lords of the First, Eighth and Tenth strong and conjoined with or aspected by one or more benefics: Long life, provided they are not also conjoined with Saturn. If only two of the above lords fulfill this condition, the life-span is medium, and if only one does so, it implies a short life.

6. The lord of the Eighth posited in an evil house or in a malefic's sign and conjoined with a malefic: Short life.

7. The lord of the Eighth in an angle, trine, or the Third, Eighth or Eleventh from the Ascendant in a benefic's sign, conjoined with or aspected by a benefic: Long life.

8. The lord of the First in the Eighth, while the lord of the Eighth is conjoined with or aspected by a malefic, both the Eighth lord

and the associated malefic being combust or in an enemy's sign or the Sixth: Short life.

9. The lord of the Eighth exalted in an angle or trine, or the lord of the Eighth in the Eighth and the lord of the First in the First, both conjoined with or aspected by benefics: Long life.

10. The lord of the Twelfth strong in his own sign and aspected by one or more benefics: A long and happy life.

For longevity and health or sickness, always note whether the Sun is strong by location and position and conjoined with or aspected by benefics. These confer good health and longevity. A weak Sun, ill-placed, conjoined with or aspected by malefics does the opposite.

HEART AND MIND

The detailed delineations in the earlier chapters which deal with the conjunctions and aspects of planets throw sufficient light on the qualities of heart and mind. What we give below are some special combinations:

1. The lord of the First strong, conjoined with and/or aspected by a benefic, promotes the affairs of whichever house it occupies. If it occupies the Second or Eleventh, wealth and income will increase; in the Third it benefits all Third house affairs; in the Fourth it will act as an incentive to the acquisition of lands or houses; in the Seventh it is favorable for matrimony; in the Ninth, for spirituality and general prosperity; and in the Tenth, for status. In the Sixth, prospects in service are bettered, and in the Eighth it contributes to longevity. In the Twelfth the native spends more than usual on personal comforts and is likely to go abroad. If the lord of the First is a natural benefic, then when it is conjoined with or aspected by benefics the native has good and benevolent intentions, but if it is a natural malefic conjoined with or aspected by malefics, the native works hard, is capable of putting up with great stress and strain, but is not soft at heart — though he may be courageous and sometimes malevolent. These principles should also be applied to the First house itself and to planets tenanting the First house. The Ascendant is the physical personality and the Moon the psyche. The traits of temper and character, capacity, steadfastness, a fickle or stable disposition — all these are indicated by the individual nature of the planets conjoined with or aspecting the First house, the lord of the First house, and the Moon.

2. If the lord of the First is a malefic located in an enemy's sign and conjoined with Saturn, Rahu or Ketu in the Sixth, Eighth or Twelfth, the native is of low conduct.

3. The lord of the Eighth, if malefic, conjoined with or aspected by a malefic: Outwardly friendly but vicious at heart.

4. The lord of the Eighth exalted, in a friend's sign, or in its own navamsha in the Fourth aspected by a benefic: Open hearted and frank.

5. The lord of the Fourth strong, conjoined with or aspected by a benefic, and the Fourth house free from malefic influence: Calm and of pure heart.

6. The lords of the Fourth and Tenth strong and conjoined in the Eleventh: Very industrious, always making efforts for increasing income.

7. The lord of the Third conjoined with (1) the Sun: chivalrous (2) the Moon: persevering (3) Mars: unintelligent, wicked and of fiery temper (4) Mercury: a pure and benevolent turn of mind (5) Jupiter: very virtuous and having many good qualities, learned, even-tempered and persevering (6) Venus: amorous and likely to enter into many quarrels and disputes as a result of the frustration of his carnal desires (7) Saturn: dull (8) Rahu: apprehensive (9) Ketu: ill-health, susceptibility to heart disease.

8. Mars in conjunction with a strong planet: Much strength and stamina.

9. The lord of the Third in a benefic's navamsha, conjoined with and aspected by a benefic: Patience and perseverance, especially if he is in an angle or trine.

10. The lord of the Third in an evil house, conjoined with or aspcted by a malefic: Very easily upset.

11. The lord of the Third conjoined with Mars in a malefic's sign: Timid.

12. A benefic in the Second aspected by another benefic: Sweet speech.

13. A malefic in the Second aspected by another malefic: Harsh speech (include Rahu and Ketu among the malefics).

14. The lord of the Second and Jupiter together in the Eighth impair one's speech, unless Jupiter or the other planet is exalted or in its own sign or navamsha.

15. The lord of the Second, if a benefic, conjoined with another benefic in an angle, both strong: The native is eloquent, particularly if the planet conjoining is Mercury.

16. Mercury strong in a good house and conjoined with or aspected by a benefic makes one eloquent.

17. The lord of the Second, Mercury and Jupiter conjoined in the Eighth are a detriment to learning unless one of them is strong by sign or navamsha.

18. Mars in the Second conjoined with a benefic, with the conjunction aspected by Mercury or Mercury occupying an angle (from the Ascendant): The native is a mathematician.

19. If the rising sign is Cancer, Libra or Pisces and the lord of the Second is aspected by Jupiter and Venus, the native excels in logic.

20. If Scorpio or Aquarius is rising and Jupiter is strong and aspected by the Sun and Venus, the native is a grammarian and well-versed in etymology.

21. Venus exalted in the Second and aspected by Jupiter: Same effect as above.

22. The lord of the Fourth in the Fourth conjoined with or aspected by a benefic: Good education, especially if Mercury is also strong.

23. The lord of the Fourth in an evil house conjoined with a malefic, aspected by a malefic: Poor education.

24. The lord of the First conjoined with Mercury in the First or Fourth house, both strong and aspected by benefics and unaspected by malefics: Learned.

25. The lord of the First and Fourth conjoined in the First or Fourth house, both strong and unaspected by malefics: Same results as above.

The Sanskrit works written in South India in olden times state that education is to be judged from the Fourth house, but in North India it is judged from the Fifth. India is one, but there have been various schools of philosophy and religious worship, various laws governing inheritance, marriage, etc. Marrying one's mother's brother's daughter is a common and religiously accepted practice in the south, even among Brahmins, but in northern India one would condemn it as the greatest sin and sacrilege. So no wonder there are different schools of astrology. The Western system takes the tropical zodiac as its basis while Hindu astrology advocates and follows the sidereal system, yet each system banks on its own assumptions and glorifies them.

In olden times higher education was mostly confined to the Brahmins, and Jaimini (a sage who flourished more than two thousand years ago and is deemed an authority on Mimansa — one of the six systems of Hindu philosophy — and who was an authoritative writer on predictive astrology as well) allocates particular planets to particular branches of learning.[1] But education is no longer confined to the six subjects of philosophy, grammar, literature, logic, etc. Many new disciplines have arisen, and technical education with all its multifarious branches has enlarged the academic jurisdiction to such an extent that it is no longer possible to use the older guidelines.

To revert to the general rule, education is judged in Northern India from the Fifth house,[2] its lord, and the planets tenanting or aspecting that house or its lord. Of course Mercury and Jupiter have a strong say in regard to intelligence and learning. Some astrologers have made a subtle distinction between learning and intelligence, the former to be judged from the Fourth and the latter from the Fifth. We do come across people who are not learned but who are very intelligent. No wonder that this is particularly so in India where many adults are illiterate. We also come across people who are learned but cannot be called particularly intelligent: some may have a mind which is good at retaining information but not quick to grasp; others may have the power of deep thinking, but are not quick in picking things up; some can follow the rules admirably but do not have the mental flexibility to analyze, discriminate, adapt or invent. But an analysis of mental faculties is too vast a subject for discussion here. To return to various types of mental aptitude and inclinations:

26. Mars and Mercury conjoined in Pisces in the Tenth: Inclined to spiritual advancement and success therein, especially if Jupiter or Saturn aspects.

---

1   See pages 39–40 of the *Jaimini Padyamritam.*
2   See page 17, *Jataka Bharana,* Bombay edition.

27. The lord of the Tenth in an angle conjunct with Venus: Bathing in holy waters (i.e. visiting ancient places of worship or sacred sites).

28. The lord of the First and Tenth conjoined: Religiously inclined and performs acts of religious merit.

29. Mercury, Jupiter and the lord of the Tenth all strong and aspected by a benefic: Performs acts of religious merit (i.e. yajnas — sacred rites with oblations to the gods).

30. The lord of the Tenth in exaltation and in conjunction with Mercury: Same effects as above.

31. All the angles holding malefics (including Rahu and Ketu) which are not in their own houses nor in exaltation, and which are not aspected by benefics: Sinful conduct and poor; not intelligent; attached to others' wives, but sometimes a favorite of the king.

RELATIONS, FRIENDS AND ENEMIES

Here we are giving some chosen aphorisms having a bearing on one's father, mother, brothers (or sisters), sons, friends and enemies. In south India the father is judged from the Ninth house, the arguments for this position being two. First, the texts state that the guru (religious preceptor) is to be judged from the Ninth, because the Ninth is the house of religion (we call it Dharma, which actually has a much wider connotation than the word religion). Among the Brahmins (who have authored most of the books on astrology, though other castes also took this up in later periods), one's father is one's first religious preceptor or guru, who initiates his son at the time of the thread ceremony. Second, the First house (significator of the native or "self") is fifth (the house governing the son) from the Ninth. But in northern India, the Tenth is regarded as the house governing the father. Each school goes by its own tradition, but both schools concur in regards to the Sun being the significator for the father, the Moon for the mother, Mars for brothers, and Jupiter for sons. Mercury is a significator for the maternal uncle and also for friends, and Mars and Saturn for enemies. One Sanskrit commentator has posed a very interesting question: Why should Mars be a significator for brothers, a positive feature of life, and also for enemies, a negative feature? He resolves the question by stating that brothers and brothers' sons are our natural enemies in the sense that they may contest an inheritance. We shall now give some important configurations involving conjunctions and aspects:

1. The lord of the First conjoined with the lord of the Fifth in the Fifth, or the lord of the First conjoined with the lord of the Ninth in the Ninth: The native's father becomes illustrious.

2. The lords of the Fourth and Sixth conjoined in the Ninth: The native's father is profligate.

3. The lord of the Tenth strong in an angle or trine and aspected by a benefic: The father is long-lived.

4. The Sun well-placed and well-aspected: Good for longevity of the father.

5. The lords of the Fourth and Ninth (jointly or severally) in the Sixth, Eighth or Twelfth and the Sun and Moon both conjoined with or aspected by malefics: Early demise of parents.

6. The Sun in debilitation aspected by a malefic: Premature death of the father, or the native is inimical to his father.

7. Mars or Saturn in the Tenth aspected by a malefic: Premature death of the father, or the native does not get on well with him.

Note: In Hindu astrology, the premature death of a parent or parents is considered in detail on the basis of the Moon's radical longitude. That being outside the scope of this book, the rules are not given here.

8. A strong Venus or Moon (Venus by location and position, and the Moon by location, position and digital strength) in a benefic's own or exalted navamsha and aspected by a benefic: Good for longevity of the mother.

9. The Moon and the lord of the Fourth conjoined together in the Fourth: The mother is long-lived.

10. The lord of the Fourth in an enemy's sign or debilitated, and a malefic in the Fourth, neither of the two conjoined with or aspected by a benefic: Early death of the mother.

11. The Fourth house hemmed in between malefics, the lord of the Fourth in an enemy's sign or debilitation, and the Moon conjoined with a malefic: Early death of mother.

12. The lord of the Fourth weak in the Sixth or Eighth and aspected by a malefic, and a malefic aspected by a malefic in the First: Premature death of the mother.

13. The lord of the Fourth and the Ascendant as well as the Moon in the Sixth, Eighth or Twelfth (severally or jointly) conjoined with Rahu/Ketu or a malefic: Early death of the mother.

14. The Moon weak in digital strength conjoined with a malefic in the Sixth, Eighth or Twelfth and a malefic in the Fourth: Early loss of the mother.

15. The lord of the Sixth conjoined with the Moon and Mars in the Sixth: The mother's conduct may not be good (*Jataka Parijata* Chapter 12, verse 71).

16. The Sun and Rahu together in the Fourth: Same as above.

17. The lord of the First conjoined with the lord of the Third in the First: The native's sibling is illustrious, particularly if Sagittarius is the rising sign.

18. The lord of the Third and Mars together, both strong and conjoined in a good house: Same result as above.

Example: Gemini rising, with the Sun (lord of the Third) and Mars together in Aries in the Eleventh.

19. A malefic in the Third aspected by another malefic: Loss of one's sibling.

20. A benefic in the Third aspected by another benefic: One's siblings prosper and the native has amicable relations with them.

21. A malefic in an angle or trine as counted from the Third house (i.e. the Sixth, Seventh, Ninth, Eleventh or Twelfth from the Ascendant) and aspected by another malefic: Loss of a sibling. But if, instead of a malefic, there is a benefic there and it is aspected by another benefic: Siblings prosper.

22. The lords of the Third and Fourth conjoined in the Fourth: Not many siblings.

23. The lords of the Third and Fourth conjoined with Mars: The native is blessed with younger siblings.

24. The lord of the First and Third conjoined: Good for younger siblings and for a fraternal relationship with them, especially if the conjunction is in the First or Third house.

25. Jupiter in the Third aspected by Venus: Happiness from siblings.

26. A conjunction of malefics (unless one of these is in its own house or lord of the Ascendant) in the Third is evil for siblings.

27. Venus in the Third aspected by Jupiter: Same result as in 25 above.

28. A benefic in the Third aspected by the Sun: Unfavorable for siblings.

29. A benefic in the Fifth aspected by another benefic gives children. The Sun, Mars and Jupiter are males; the Moon and Venus are females; Mercury is a male eunuch and Saturn is a female eunuch. The odd signs Aries, Gemini, Leo, Libra, Sagittarius and Aquarius are male signs, while the even signs Taurus, Cancer, Virgo, Scorpio, Capricorn and Pisces are female. The sign on the Fifth house and the planet or planets tenanting or aspecting the Fifth, whether male or female, will determine whether there will be more sons or daughters.

30. The lord of the Fifth conjoined with or aspected by a malefic is an unfavorable factor, particularly so if in the Sixth, Eighth or Twelfth, which are called the evil houses.

31. The lord of the Fifth in a good house[3] conjoined with a benefic or aspected by a benefic promotes happiness in respect to children.

32. Whether or not Jupiter is the lord of the Fifth, examine him. A strong Jupiter, well-placed, conjoined with or aspected by a benefic is a plus factor, while a weak Jupiter in an evil house conjoined with or aspected by a malefic is a minus factor regarding children. But if the conjoining or aspecting malefic is the lord of the First or Fifth, he is not evil.

33. Mars in the Fifth aspected by a malefic causes repeated loss of children, but if, instead of a malefic, Jupiter aspects such a Mars, only the first child will be lost; subsequent children will live.

34. The lords of the Fifth, Seventh and Ninth in the Sixth, Eighth or Twelfth (severally or jointly, or by way of one planet in one of these houses and the other two in another) and the Fifth house aspected by a malefic: No son.

---

3   All houses other than the evil houses, i.e. the Sixth, Eighth and Twelfth, are good houses.

35. The Moon and Venus together in the Sixth: One son.

36. The Sun conjoined with Venus in the First or Seventh: No son due to the wife being barren.

37. A benefic tenanting the Fifth house and aspected by a benefic: Several children.

38. The lord of the Fifth in an angle or trine, in a benefic's sign and conjoined with a benefic: The birth of a son comparatively early in life.

39. The lords of the Second and Fifth weak and aspected by a malefic, and the Fifth house also aspected by a malefic: No children.

40. The lord of the Fifth well-placed and Jupiter aspecting him or the Fifth house: The birth of a son or sons.

41. The Fifth house and its lord conjoined with or aspected by a benefic: The birth of children.

42. The lords of the First and Fifth conjoined with and aspected by a benefic: The birth of children.

43. If the Moon in the Tenth aspects malefics in the Fourth and Venus occupies the Seventh (from the Ascendant): There may be no continuity in the male line.

44. The lord of the First in the Sixth or Eighth, and the lord of the Fifth conjoined with a malefic and aspected by his enemy or a planet in debilitation: Loss of a child.

45. A malefic in the Fifth, with the lord of the Fifth debilitated and not aspected by a benefic: No children.

46. Jupiter in Cancer, Sagittarius, Aquarius or Pisces in the Fifth unaspected by any other planet: A son is acquired, though with difficulty.

47. If the fifth house from the Ascendant, the fifth from the Moon and the fifth from Jupiter are all tenanted by malefics and unaspected by benefics: No children.

48. A malefic in the Fifth and the lord of the Fifth hemmed in between malefics and not conjoined with or aspected by a benefic: No children.

49. The lord of the Fifth weak, not conjoined with or aspected by a benefic, and Jupiter hemmed in between malefics: No children.

50. The lords of the Fifth and Seventh, Mars and Jupiter conjoined: Loss of children.

51. The Sun in the Eighth aspected by Mars in the Ascendant, and the Fourth house aspected by a benefic: A son is born late in the native's life.

52. Saturn in the First, Jupiter in the Eighth, and Mars in the Twelfth aspected by two benefics: Same as above.

Now follow some aphorisms which have a bearing on one's relatives.

53. (1) If the lord of the Fourth is a benefic and is aspected by another benefic and (2) the Moon and Mercury are strong, the native is much respected by his kinsmen.

According to Parashara, clause (2) should be "if the Moon is in the Ascendant."

54. If there is a malefic in the Fourth conjunct a debilitated or combust planet, and no benefic conjoins or aspects the Fourth house, the native is at loggerheads with his kinsmen.

55. The lord of the Fourth strong in an angle or trine and aspected by a benefic: The native benefits his relations.

Now we give some combinations concerning friends and enemies. In Hindu astrology friends are judged from the Fourth, while in the Western system from the Eleventh.

56. The lord of the Fourth, if itself a benefic and aspected by a benefic, gives good friends.

57. The lord of the Fourth exalted in the Ninth or Eleventh and conjoined with the lord of the First: Gain from friends.

58. Mercury well-placed by sign and house and conjoined with Venus: Good friends.

59. Mercury strong in the Second, Ninth or Eleventh, not conjoined with or aspected by a malefic, but having the aspect of Jupiter: Benefit from friends.

60. Mars in The Sixth aspected by Saturn gives a number of enemies.

61. A benefic in the Sixth conjoined with or aspected by another benefic does not give much trouble or create much apprehension from enemies.

62. The lord of the First conjoined with two malefics, one on each side: Always in dread of an enemy.

63. A benefic in the Sixth conjoined with or aspected by another benefic: No fear from enemies.

64. A malefic in the Sixth conjoined with or aspected by another malefic: Wounds, fear from enemies.

65. The lord of the Sixth weak, hemmed in between two malefics: Trouble from enemies.

66. The lord of the Sixth weak and aspected by an enemy: Same result as above.

67. The lord of the Sixth in the Eighth or Twelfth, combust or in an enemy's sign, and the lord of the First in an angle or trine in its own or a friend's sign and aspected by a benefic: Destruction of one's foes.

68. Apart from the lord of the Sixth house, Mars and Saturn are significators for the Sixth. If they are strong and well aspected, the native conquers his enemies, but if they are weak and aspected by malefics the native is oppressed by his enemies.

69. The Sun is the significator of the self. Thus the Sun well located by sign or navamsha and well posited and aspected signifies that the native overcomes his enemies.

70. The First house stands for the self and the Sixth for enemies and sickness. Thus Mantreshwara says that if the lord of the Sixth is weak (due to combustion, location or position) but there is a benefic in the Sixth and the lord of the First is stronger than the lord of the Sixth, the enemy is annihilated. A variation of this same principle is in 67 above.

In Western astrology open enemies are judged from the Seventh house and secret enemies from the Twelfth. Not so in Hindu astrology, where we judge all enemies, as well as sickness, from the Sixth. There is no distinction between open and secret enemies here. Of course, a planet in the Twelfth will affect the Sixth by reflex action because any planet in the Twelfth will fully aspect the Sixth house.

MARRIAGE AND "THE PLEASURES OF THE BED"

Marriage and the pleasures of sex are related, and yet at times they act, so to say, on different planes. The Seventh house governs both marriage and sex. The Twelfth house determines "the pleasures of the bed." Hindu astrologers use terms such as "comforts of the bed" or "pleasures of the bed" to denote romantic relationships which are not infrequently extramarital. Many people never marry, whether by their own volition or due to the compulsion of events and circumstances, and yet many of them enjoy a more abundant sex life than the ordinary married person. Here readers will note that "enjoy" is used in a particular restricted sense. When the Seventh house is weak or the Seventh lord afflicted, one has little conjugal happiness and married life not infrequently becomes a bed of thorns rather than roses, but if the Twelfth house and Venus are strong there is no dearth of enjoyment. If the Seventh is strong but the Twelfth house weak and afflicted there may be perfect compatibility between the couple but little enjoyment. One party may be in ill health, or a man may have to live away from his wife or be so frequently overworked, mentally upset or physically tired that he has little time, energy or inclination for marital enjoyment.

Besides the Seventh and Twelfth houses, Venus is the planet of enjoyment in general and sex in particular. These three factors, if strong, beneficially conjoined and well aspected, offer maximum opportunities; these three weak and afflicted, conjoined with or aspected by malefics, deny pleasure and not infrequently cause immense misery and frustration. In delineation we have generally used the pronoun "he" for the native and the noun "wife" for the native's partner. But the aphorisms below may be applied to female nativities also. To begin with:

1. The Moon, Mercury, Jupiter and Venus — two or more of these conjoined in the Seventh give a good-looking and clever wife.

2. Venus in the Seventh aspected by a malefic may make the wife wayward.

3. Mercury in Taurus in the Seventh, not conjoined with or aspected by a benefic but aspected by a malefic: Unfavorable for the longevity of the wife.

4. Jupiter in Capricorn in the Seventh, not conjoined with or aspected by any benefic but aspected by Mars: More than one wife.

5. Venus in Scorpio in the Seventh, not conjoined with or aspected by a benefic but aspected by Saturn: Unfavorable for the wife's longevity.

6. Saturn in Pisces in the Seventh, aspected by the Sun: Unfavorable for the wife's longevity.

7. A conjunction of malefics in the Seventh house: Unfavorable for matrimonial happiness. The *Phala Deepika,* a standard work, states an exception: "If Mars and Saturn be conjoined in Cancer in the Seventh house the wife is chaste and beautiful."[4]

8. Moon and Saturn together in the Seventh: Probability of re-marriage.

9. Saturn in the Seventh aspected by Venus: Excessive cupidity.

10. Venus in the Seventh aspected by Mars or Saturn: Same as above.

11. The Sun in the Seventh in a female nativity, aspected by an enemy: Separation from husband.

12. The lord of the Seventh in an enemy's sign or debilitated and aspected by a malefic: Evil for matrimonial happiness, particularly if in an evil house.

13. Venus in an enemy's sign or debilitated and aspected by a malefic: Same as above, particularly if in the Sixth or Eighth.

14. Even a malefic in his own sign in the Seventh is good, especially if conjoined with or aspected by a benefic.

15. A conjunction of the Moon and Venus fully aspected by a conjunction of Mars and Saturn: Unhappiness due to one's wife or children (no wife and children or misery on their account).

16. If Mercury or Saturn is in the Seventh and there is a conjunction of two planets in the the Eleventh: Two marriages.

17. Even a benefic in the Seventh is not good if he happens to be the lord of the Sixth, Eighth or Twelfth and aspected by a malefic.

---

4   Chapter 10, verse 3.

Note: For a Scorpio Ascendant, Venus in the Seventh is not bad despite its lordship of the Twelfth, because it will be in its own sign, Taurus.

18. The Moon and Venus together in the Seventh, particularly in Taurus, Cancer or Libra, give several wives or great enjoyment of sex (polygamy was formerly very common, and such aphorisms have to be adapted to modern conditions).

19. A conjunction of Mars and Venus in the Fifth, Seventh or Ninth: Ill health to one's wife; unsatisfied lust on the part of the native.

20. If Taurus, Cancer, Leo or Libra is the Ascendant and Venus in the Seventh is aspected by Mars and/or Saturn: The native and his wife are both wanton.

21. Mercury and Venus together in the Seventh aspected by a benefic: Late marriage. (An old authority, Kalyan Varma, states it, but we beg to differ.)

22. The lord of the Tenth and his navamsha dispositor (i.e. if a planet is in Libra navamsha then Venus would be his navamsha dispositor) conjoined with or aspected by Saturn and also aspected by the lord of the Sixth: Many wives (in modern, non-polygamous societies, the native may enjoy many women).

23. Mercury and Venus conjoined in the Twelfth: Pleasures of sex.

24. Venus in the Twelfth aspected by a benefic: Same as above.

25. The lord of the Twelfth exalted and aspected by a benefic: Pleasures of the bed.

26. The lord of the Seventh in the First conjoined with a benefic: Wife from a good family.

27. The lord of the Seventh exalted, tenanting an angle, and aspected by the lord of the Tenth: Several wives (in ancient times, it was considered good fortune to have several wives).

28. The lord of the Seventh in an angle in a benefic's sign and aspected by a benefic: Good wife.

29. The lord of the Second or Seventh conjoined with Venus, either in the Sixth, Eighth or Twelfth and in conjunction with a malefic: Loss of wife.

30. If Venus is not conjoined with or aspected by a benefic, and there is a malefic in the fourth from Venus and another malefic in the eighth from Venus: Loss of wife.

31. If Venus is hemmed in between malefics (Example: Venus at 20° Virgo with one malefic at 15° Virgo and another malefic at 26°, so that Venus is sandwiched between the two) and not conjoined with or aspected by a benefic: Same as above.

32. If Venus is at 20° Virgo with malefic 'A' in Leo and another malefic 'B' in Libra, and if there is no planet other than Venus between 'A' and 'B', then Venus would be deemed hemmed in between malefics.

33. The Sun and Venus conjoined in the Fifth, Seventh or Ninth: The native's wife suffers infirmity in some limb.

34. If, in a female nativity, a weak malefic is in the Seventh aspected by a benefic, the husband forsakes the wife; if the malefic planet is in debilitation, she will be inimical to her husband.

35. A malefic in the Seventh, aspected by another malefic: A wicked wife.

36. The lord of the First is a malefic and occupies the Seventh alone and unaspected by a benefic: Wife from a low family.

37. A conjunction of malefics in the Second and the lord of the Seventh aspected by or conjoined with a malefic: Premature death of wife.

38. If Mercury is the lord of the Seventh and conjoined with a malefic in debilitation or an enemy's sign or navamsha in the Sixth or Eighth, hemmed in between malefics and aspected by a malefic: The wife kills her husband (many a wife is responsible for killing her husband by resorting to constant quarrels but is not called a murderess in the eyes of the law).

39. Venus in the Seventh aspected by or conjoined with a malefic (including Rahu and Ketu): Adulterous.

40. The lord of the Seventh conjoined with Rahu or Ketu: Adulterous.

41. The lord of the Seventh is a benefic and the Seventh house is aspected by benefics: Not adulterous.

42. The lord of the Seventh in the Sixth, Eighth or Twelfth in a malefic's sign, conjoined with and/or aspected by a malefic: Little matrimonial happiness.

43. The lord of the Seventh in a malefic's sign and conjoined with Venus: Over-sexed.

44. The lords of the Second, Sixth and Seventh and Venus conjoined in the Ascendant: Over-sexed.

Note: The *Sarvarth Chintamani,* another standard work, adds that if a malefic conjoins the above conjunction the native is very adulterous, but if the conjunction is aspected by a benefic he is not so.

45. The lords of the First and Sixth conjoined with Venus and a malefic: Same as in 44 above.

46. The lords of the First, Second and Sixth conjoined with a malefic in the Seventh: Liaisons with others' wives.

47. The lords of the Sixth and Seventh conjoined with a malefic in the Ninth: Excessive sexual craving.

48. A conjunction of the lords of the First and Sixth and a malefic: Attached to others' wives.

49. The lords of the First, Second and Sixth conjoined with a malefic in the Seventh: Very adulterous.

50. The lords of the Second, Seventh and Tenth conjoined in the Tenth: Liaisons with other women.

51. The Moon and Venus conjoined in the Seventh: Attached to several women.

52. Mercury and Jupiter conjoined in the Seventh: Same as above.

53. Mars and Venus together in the Fifth, Seventh or Ninth: No happiness as regards the native's wife; liaisons with others.

54. A malefic in the First aspected by another malefic in the Seventh (not in its own sign or exaltation), a malefic in the Twelfth and a weak Moon in the Fifth: No happiness in respect to wife and son.

55. The lord of the Third conjoined with Venus in an angle or trine, both planets strong: Much virility and capacity for sexual enjoyment.

56. The Moon or Venus conjoined with Mars, Saturn or Rahu in the Ninth house: Amorous with the wife of a senior (i.e. religious preceptor, uncle, etc.).

The astrological aphorisms in regard to marriage given in this chapter are based on the evaluation of a single chart — husband's or wife's. But there is a vast literature in the standard works giving detailed instructions on how to compare the two charts to determine if there is mutual compatibility between them and if they would make a good husband and wife to each other. It is the usual practice in the orthodox community to have the birth charts compared. The marriage is fixed only if the charts compare well.

In the Western system, the harmonious configurations between two charts are quite different than among the Hindus. Since we have dealt with the matter in detail in our other book, *Love and Marriage in Vedic Astrology*, we will not go into it here.

WEALTH, LUCK AND PROSPERITY

Now we will give some chosen aphorisms on wealth, good luck, prosperity and happiness. Strictly speaking, a person may be wealthy but not happy and vice-versa. But since money is the chief source of procuring material comforts, it is only proper that happiness should be included in the same grouping. The principal houses involved are the Second, Ninth and Eleventh. We have also included some aphorisms dealing with poverty and expenditure because that is the negative side of the subject, and no delineation is complete until both sides of the picture are presented. Of course, the First house and its lord figures in every picture because it represents the self, which feels the enjoyment or want of wealth and happiness.

1. Three benefics conjoined in the First house: High position.

2. A conjunction of three benefics in the Ascendant: A happy, contented and comfortable life.

3. A conjunction of Mercury, Jupiter and Venus in the First aspected by Saturn in the Seventh: Much happiness and enjoyment.

4. Jupiter in the First aspected by Saturn in the Seventh also gives much enjoyment in life, provided the Sun is in the Tenth.

5. A benefic in the Eighth conjoined with or aspected by another benefic: A happy and comfortable life.

6. The lord of the First conjoined with a benefic in a fixed sign,[5] and a benefic or benefics in the First house: Wealthy.

7. The lord of the Second and Eleventh conjoined in the Second or Eleventh: Wealthy, particularly so if the two are natural friends or the sign in which they conjoin happens to be the sign ruled by one and the exaltation sign of the other. Example — Pisces Ascendant, with the lord of the Second, Mars, and the lord of the Eleventh, Saturn, in Capricorn (Capricorn being the sign of Saturn and the exaltation sign of Mars).

8. The lords of the Second and Eleventh both conjoined in the Ascendant, particularly if the Ascendant is ruled by one and the exaltation sign of the other: Wealthy. Example — Capricorn Ascendant, with Mars and Saturn together in the First.

9. The lords of the First and Second together in a good house: Wealthy. It is better still if there is a conjunction of the lords of the First, Second and Eleventh. This conjunction in a good house will naturally be far better than in an evil house. Example — Sagittarius Ascendant with Jupiter, Venus and Saturn conjoined in Libra. Take into account the sign position also.

10. The lord of the First and Second in conjunction in an angle, the lord of the Second being in his own sign or in exaltation: Wealthy.

11. A conjunction of benefics in the Second house and the lord of the Second exalted: Wealthy. Example — Virgo Ascendant, with the Moon and Jupiter in the Second and the lord of the Second, Venus, exalted in Pisces in the Seventh.

12. The lords of the Second and Third together in the Ascendant: Financial gain from brothers or personal efforts.

13. The lords of the Second and Fourth together in the First: Gains from the mother and from real estate.

14. The lords of the Second and Seventh conjoined in the First: Gains from marriage or partnership.

---

5   Taurus, Leo, Scorpio and Aquarius are the fixed signs.

15. The lords of the Second and Ninth conjoined in the First: Gains from religion, law, or from overseas.

16. The lords of the Second and Tenth together in the First: Gains from the father or superiors.

17. The lords of the Second and Eleventh together in the First: Gains from friends, societies or joint stock companies.

Note: In 12 to 17 above, the ascending sign will also be a major factor in assessing the extent of wealth.

18. The Moon in the Second aspected by Venus: Wealth is augmented.

19. A benefic in the Second aspected by another: Same as above (see some exceptions given hereafter).

20. *Jataka Parijata,* Chapter 11, verse 57, uses the Sanskrit word Saumya in relation to the Second house. The word means "a benefic," but also means "Mercury." If we take it to mean Mercury, it would clash with the rule given in the Sanskrit *Nidhi,* Chapter 4, verse 2, that "if there is a malefic in the Second or Mercury tenants the Second and is aspected by the Moon, the native is devoid of wealth." Despite the citation above that Mercury in the Second aspected by the Moon makes one indigent, we feel that because with Gemini rising this would be the aspect of the lord of the Second on the lord of the First and with Virgo rising it will be the lord of the Eleventh aspecting the Ascendant lord, it cannot under such circumstances be called evil.

21. The Moon weak in digital strength (particularly on the fourteenth or fifteenth day of the dark fortnight) in the Second, if aspected by Mercury, leads to loss of wealth.

22. Venus in the Second conjoined with or aspected by a benefic makes one wealthy, especially if Aquarius is rising.

23. The Sun and Moon together in the Second: Not much wealth, unless Cancer is the rising sign.

24. The lord of the Second and Eleventh conjoined: Wealthy, especially if aspected by a benefic.

25. Saturn in the Second aspected by the Moon: Wealthy.

26. Venus in the Second aspected by the Moon: Wealthy.

27. The Moon and Saturn conjoined in the Fourth, Tenth or Eleventh: Wealthy.

28. The Moon in Cancer (but not in its debilitated navamsha, which is Scorpio) aspected by Jupiter and Venus: Wealthy and famous.

29. The lord of the First and Ninth together in the First or Ninth, conjoined with or aspected by Jupiter: Good luck throughout life.

30. The lord of the First conjoined with a malefic in the Eighth, if unaspected by a benefic: Little happiness.

31. A planet debilitated, in an enemy's sign, or combust in the Ninth makes one devoid of good name, wealth and religious merit. A malefic in the above condition is worse than a benefic. If the lord of the Ninth or a benefic aspects the above planet, the evil is mitigated, but a malefic's aspect augments the evil.

32. A benefic or a malefic in exaltation, its own sign, or in a great friend's sign is good for luck, particularly if aspected by the lord of the First or Ninth or a benefic.

33. The lord of the Ninth, well placed and conjoined with or aspected by a benefic, augments good luck.

34. The lord of the Ninth, ill located, ill posited, and conjoined with or aspected by a malefic, pulls down one's luck and prosperity.

Note: The dispositor of the lord of the Ninth should also be assessed on the lines indicated above, for he also has a great say in the matter of good luck, prosperity and analogous inferences drawn.

35. The Moon in the Ninth aspected by Mars, Mercury and Saturn: Great good luck.

36. An exalted planet in the Ninth aspected by a benefic: A king.

37. A conjunction of benefics in the First, Second or Eleventh brings in much money. The stronger the benefics, the more money they will bring.

38. A benefic in the First, Second or Eleventh, aspected by another benefic, will also be conducive to gain. (Some exceptions have been noted in this book.)

39. If the Sun is in Aries or the Tenth house aspected by a benefic, the native earns much by his personal efforts.

40. A benefic in the Twelfth conjoined with or aspected by another benefic, with the lord of the Twelfth weak in debilitation: Not many expenditures (i.e. accumulation of wealth).

41. The lord of the Twelfth strong and a weak planet in the Twelfth aspected by a malefic: Heavy expenditures (therefore loss of money).

42. The Sun and Moon conjoined in the Twelfth: Loss of wealth due to the king (i.e. income tax, customs penalty, etc.).

43. Mars in the Twelfth aspected by Mercury: Destruction of wealth in many ways.

44. Jupiter and Venus conjoined in the Twelfth: Wealth is preserved.

45. A planet in the Second, in his enemy's sign or in debilitation, combust and aspected by a malefic: Loss of wealth.

46. The lord of the Second combust in his sign of debilitation and aspected by a malefic: Poverty. The evil will be mitigated somewhat if the planet is in its own or its exalted navamsha, or in the First or Eleventh.

47. The Sun and Saturn together in the Second cause poverty.

48. Jupiter in Capricorn (unless posited between 0° and 3° 20′ or 20° and 23° 20′ or fully aspected by the Moon) makes one poor.

49. The Moon not conjoined with any planet, nor having any planet in the second, fourth, seventh, tenth or twelfth from him and unaspected by any planet, makes one poor.

50. Venus in Virgo navamsha, unless conjoined with or aspected by a benefic: Pulls one down financially.

51. A conjunction of malefics in the Second house, unless one or both planets are in exaltation or their own signs, leads to dissipation of wealth, particularly if this conjunction is aspected by a weak Moon.

52. The Sun and Mars together in the Second: Poverty and skin diseases.

53. Jupiter in the Second aspected by Mercury: Unfavorable for finances.

54. Mercury in the Second aspected by the Moon: Same as above (but note the exceptions discussed earlier).

55. A conjunction of three malefics (including Rahu and Ketu) in the First house: Sorrowful and miserable.

Note: For wealth always consider Jupiter. A Jupiter strong by sign and well-placed in a good house, aspected by or conjoined with a benefic or benefics, confers wealth. An afflicted Jupiter does the opposite. What is affliction? To be weak by sign, placed in an evil house, in conjunction with or aspected by a malefic.

REAL ESTATE

Since immovable properties (i.e. real estate) and vehicles are strong adjuncts of wealth and prosperity, we will now give some selected aphorisms on these.

It will be observed that the mother, real estate, vehicles or convey-ances (and, according to the southern astrologers, even education) are judged from the Fourth house, so in these aphorisms the Fourth house and the lord of the Fourth figure again and again. If the Fourth house and its lord are afflicted, how may one distinguish whether one would suffer in respect to his mother, his real estate, vehicles or education? Conversely, if both the Fourth house and its lord are strong and conjoined with or aspected by benefics, what is the criteria to judge whether one will be happy in respect to his mother or whether he will possess real estate, vehicles, or a good education and learning?

A simple guideline for this is: Judge the Fourth house and its lord, and (a) the Moon for the mother, (b) Mars for real estate, (c) Venus for vehicles and (d) Mercury for education.

As we have noted earlier, we in Northern India judge education from the Fifth house, not from the Fourth.

1. The lord of the Ninth conjoined with Venus in the Fourth: A comfortable house.

2. The lord of the First and the Fourth in the Fourth: Sudden gain in real estate.

3. The lord of the Fourth in his own sign or navamsha aspected by Jupiter and Venus: Good for properties.

4. The lord of the Third conjoined with a benefic and the lords of the First and Fourth aspecting each other: Gain of property.

5. We have generally observed that if the lord of the Fourth is well aspected and Saturn (not in his own house or exaltation) tenants the Fourth, the native purchases an old house.

6. The lord of the Fourth in the Twelfth aspected by a benefic: Acquires old property.

7. The lord of the Fourth strong in an angle or trine and aspected by a benefic: A good and beautiful house.

8. Any strong planet in the Fourth aspected by or conjoined with a benefic: Good for properties.

9. The lord of the Tenth conjoined with a malefic in the Fourth and Eighth, without aspect of benefics: Loss of property.

10. A weak malefic in the Fourth aspected by another malefic: No property.

11. The Sun or Mars in debilitation in the Fourth house without any benefic aspect: Same as above.

12. The lords of the Second, Fourth and Twelfth in the Eighth conjoined with a malefic: Loss of property.

VEHICLES

1. The Fourth house and the lord of the Fourth both strong and aspected by benefics: Owns his own vehicle.[6]

2. The lord of the Fourth in the Fourth in the navamsha of a benefic, conjoined with Mercury and aspected by benefics: Same as above.

3. The lord of the Fourth in the First in Cancer, or any other sign if conjoined with or aspected by the Moon: Has horses.

4. The Moon in a benefic sign in the Second or Fourth, conjoined with a benefic: Has horses.

5. The lords of the First and Fourth and the Moon conjoined in the Ascendant: Has horses.

---

6   In countries like the United States where almost everyone owns a car, these yogas have to be considered as indicators of owning several cars or a luxury vehicle. Similar mental adjustments have to be made regarding the traditional references to horses and elephants.

6. The lord of the Fourth conjoined with Venus in the First: Has elephants.

7. A full Moon and Venus, both strong and conjoined in an angle or trine: Luxurious vehicles.

8. The lords of the First and Fourth, the Moon and Venus all conjoined: Luxurious vehicles.

9. The Moon, Jupiter, Venus and the lord of the Fourth together in an angle or trine: Luxurious vehicles.

10. The lord of the Fourth conjoined with Jupiter: Good conveyances.

11. The lord of the Fourth conjoined with a benefic in the Tenth: Honor and conveyances.

12. The lord of the Fourth conjoined with Mars in the Eleventh in Aries or Scorpio: Vehicles.

13. The lord of the Fourth and Ninth together in the Tenth or Eleventh: Has vehicles and is a favorite of the king.

14. The lord of the Fourth in the Ninth with Jupiter and Venus in a benefic's sign in the Ninth, and the lord of the Ninth in an angle or trine: Many vehicles and large properties.

15. If the lords of the Fourth and Tenth are both strong and both conjoined with or aspected by the lord of the Ninth: Good for conveyances and status.

16. The lord of the Fourth debilitated or in an enemy's house in the Sixth, Eighth or Twelfth, if aspected by the lord of the Ninth or Eleventh: Eventually acquires a vehicle, but after many difficulties.

STATUS AND POSITION

There are many people who are not very wealthy yet attain an eminent status. Conversely, there are many who are extremely rich yet hanker for status and dole out large amounts of money in hopes of receiving some recognition from society or the government, and who line up to obtain a title. But generally wealth and status go hand in hand. One may become eminent due to learning (poets laureate, editors of influential papers and magazines, authors, professors, inventors, prize winners in the field of science), excellence in profession (eminent doctors, lawyers, soldiers, commanders), big business, social services, religion, philosophy or politics — sometimes the eminence is so great that one becomes a central figure in his own region, state, or country or even an international figure. The kind of eminence a particular person will attain depends largely on the configuration of planets, for which the birth chart must be examined as a whole. Eminence also depends on education, heredity, environment and the sphere of work. In ancient India many of the great savants, eminent as scholars or religious leaders, were poor, but now the picture has changed. One rarely comes across an eminent person who is not fairly rich. The house primarily concerned is the Tenth, because in the scheme of houses, the Tenth is the highest — it is at the meridian. Success also depends upon the general strength of the horoscope, the placement of planets in signs and houses, and their conjunctions and aspects. Some well-tried aphorisms are given below:

1. An exalted planet in the First aspected by another exalted planet in the Seventh: Overlordship.

2. An exalted planet in the Fourth aspected by another exalted planet in the Tenth: Very exalted position.

3. If both 1 and 2 apply: Kingship.

Note: For 1 to 3 above, still better results follow if the Moon is in Cancer.

4. If the Ascendant is *vargottama* (occupying the same navamsha as the natal ascending sign) and four or more planets aspect the Ascendant: A king. (The Moon's aspect is neither a constituent nor a denigrating factor.)

5. If the Moon is *vargottama* and four or more planets aspect the Moon: Same as above.

6. All the angles tenanted by benefics (unaspected by malefics): Intelligent, learned, wealthy and virtuous; a favorite of the king.

Since there are only four benefics, and Mercury and Venus cannot be in the tenth and fourth from each other, if three angles are tenanted by benefics and the fourth has Mars or Saturn in its own house the dictum will be fulfilled. The stronger the benefics, the better the results.

7. The lord of the Tenth, if a benefic, conjoined with and aspected by a benefic and tenanting a benefic's navamsha (but not debilitated in that navamsha): The native commands and exercises authority.

8. The lord of the Tenth, conjoined with Saturn and aspected by the lord of the Eighth, in a malefic's sign and navamsha: His orders are cruel and afflict others.

9. The lord of the Tenth conjoined with a benefic or hemmed in between benefics, and occupying a benefic's navamsha (but not debilitated in that navamsha): Occupies a respectable position and is famous.

10. The lord of the Tenth weak, conjoined with and aspected by a malefic: Unsuccessful in undertakings, fails to rise to a good position.

11. If the lord of the Seventh is a benefic and conjoined with and/or aspected by a benefic: Occupies an elevated position.

12. The lord of an angle conjoined with the lord of a trine: Good position. If the lord of an angle conjoins the lords of both the trines: Very good position. If the lords of all four angles conjoin with the lords of both the trines: Most excellent position. The results are extremely good if the conjunction takes place in a good house, preferably the Tenth, First, Ninth, Fourth, Seventh or Fifth in descending order. One important consideration is: There should be no conjunction of the lords of the Third, Sixth, Eighth or Eleventh. The association of the lords of these houses is a liability. But when one and the same planet is lord of an angle or trine and one of these four houses, it is not as unfavorable.

Note: If, instead of the conjunction stated above, there is mutual full aspect, it is treated as equally effective.

13. If Aries is rising and there is a conjunction of the Moon, Mars and Jupiter: Exalted position.

14. Mars in Capricorn in the Ascendant, fully aspected by the Moon in Cancer in the Seventh: Same effect.

15. The Sun and Moon in Aries in the Ascendant, provided the Sun is not between 20° and 23° 20' and the Moon is not between 23° 20' and 26° 40': Very eminent status.

16. If there is a conjunction of the Moon, Mercury and Venus in Taurus in the Eleventh house and the Sun is in Aries and Jupiter in exaltation in the First: A king.

17. Any one planet in its sign of exaltation, provided it is also in its exalted navamsha and aspected by a strong friendly planet: Exalted position.

The Sun in 0° to 3° 20′ Aries, the Moon in 13° 20′ to 16° 40′ Taurus, Mars in 0° to 3° 20′ Capricorn, Jupiter in 0° to 3° 20′ Cancer, Venus in 26° 40′ to 30° Pisces and Saturn in 0° to 3° 20′ Libra are exalted by navamsha as well as by sign. Mercury is exalted in 0° to 15° Virgo by sign and 26° 40′ to 30° by navamsha. Therefore the two do not synchronize.

18. In 17 above, if the planet is in its sign of exaltation and its own navamsha and aspected by a friendly planet: Good status.

19. A benefic in the Ascendant and the lord of the First in an angle aspected by three friends: High position.

20. If the Moon at 3° Taurus is in the Ascendant and aspected by Venus, and the malefics are conjoined in the Third or Sixth, or some in the Third, others in the Sixth: Good position.

21. The lord of the First in the First, aspected by three planets located in a friend's sign: Very good for high rank.

22. The full Moon in Aries navamsha, fully aspected by Jupiter, raises one to a very high position provided that the Moon is not aspected by any other planet and no planet is in its sign of debilitation.

23. The full Moon in the Third, Sixth, Tenth or Eleventh, aspected by Jupiter, makes one a king, provided that the Moon is not aspected by any other planet and the dispositor of the Moon is in the Seventh or Tenth.

24. The full Moon in Leo navamsha confers a very exalted position, provided that benefics unconjoined with malefics are conjunct in angles from the Ascendant.

25. If the full Moon is in Cancer between 0° and 3° 20′ or in Taurus between 13° 20′ and 16° 40′ and a strong benefic aspects it while no malefic tenants the First house, the native occupies a kingly position.

26. The Moon in Taurus aspected by Jupiter: High position.

27. The Sun, Moon and Venus conjoined with and aspected by Jupiter: Same as above.

28. If Jupiter is in 13° 20′ to 16° 40′ Cancer, in 0° to 3° 20′ or 23° 20′ to 26° 40′ Sagittarius or 13° 20′ to 16° 40′ Pisces, aspected

by Mars with the Sun in Aries, the native, though born in a poor family, rises very high in life.

29. A full Moon, Mercury, Jupiter or Venus in the Ninth house, and not combust and aspected by friends: The native attains a high position.

30. Jupiter in the Fifth aspected by the lord of the Fifth raises the native to an exalted status provided Venus is in Pisces.

31. Mars in Capricorn aspected by the Sun, Moon and Jupiter: Kingly position.

32. Jupiter in the Ascendant, in any sign except Capricorn, aspected by a benefic: Good position.

33. The lord of the Ascendant in its sign of exaltation and aspecting the Moon: High rank.

34. Venus in its own sign or exalted, aspected by Jupiter: Same as above.

35. The Moon in Taurus fully aspecting Mercury and Venus: Exalted position.

36. The Sun in a great friend's sign and in his own or his exalted navamsha aspected by the Moon: Overlordship.

37. The Sun in 0° to 3° 20' or 13° 20' to 16° 40' Aries conjoined with the Moon in 3° 20' to 6° 40' or 10° to 13° 20' Aries: Elevated position.

38. The Moon and Jupiter together in Cancer: Rich and occupying a high status.

39. Mercury, Jupiter and Venus conjoined in the Second from the Sun, provided all three are free from combustion: Kingly position.

40. A full Moon aspected by its dispositor, Venus, and a benefic is a very good configuration for riches and position, provided that the Moon is not conjoined with or aspected by a malefic.

41. Jupiter and Venus together in the Second: Good position and wealth.

42. A full Moon in Pisces aspected by friends: Elevated rank.

43. A full Moon aspected by its dispositor in exaltation: Good name and fame. This is possible only when the Moon is in Aries

aspected by Mars in Capricorn, or in Pisces aspected by Jupiter in Cancer. The effects will be much better if both the Moon and Jupiter are in their own or exalted navamshas also.

44. Profession should be judged by (a) the position of the lord of the First, (b) planets in the tenth houses from the Ascendant, Sun and Moon, (c) the lords of the tenth houses from the Ascendant, Sun and Moon and (d) the navamsha dispositors of (c) above. Each planet is a significator for particular affairs. Planets referred to in (c) and (d) above also indicate, through their conjunctions and aspects, the type of work the native is likely to undertake — e.g. the lord of the Tenth conjoined with Mercury indicates a merchant or trader. Many and various types of work are being developed every day. The planets are only seven and the professions many, hence the native's background, education, equipment and financial resources must be taken into account.

45. In determining a career of service and a rise in status, the Sixth house and the lord thereof also have a great say, as well as the Third house and its lord, though in lesser measure.

46. A Scorpio Ascendant or Moon in Scorpio, as well as planets in the Sixth, indicate service, particularly the lord of the First or Tenth in the Sixth.

Note: Look for conjunctions of the lords of the Third and Sixth with other planets, and whether these have aspects from benefics.

47. If the birth is on the fourteenth or fifteenth day of the dark fortnight (i.e. the Moon within 24° of the Sun and applying to him) and the Moon at 26° 40' to 30° of a cardinal sign, 23° 20' to 26° 40' of a fixed sign, or 0° to 3° 20' of a mutable sign,[7] such a Moon not being aspected by any planet, then the good effects of many configurations indicating royalty, wealth and high position are nullified.

48. Malefics in an enemy's sign or in debilitation in the angles and a conjunction of benefics in the Sixth, Eighth or Twelfth destroy the good effects of other favorable configurations.

---

7   Aries, Cancer, Libra and Capricorn are cardinal or movable; Taurus, Leo, Scorpio and Aquarius are fixed; and Gemini, Virgo, Sagittarius and Pisces are mutable or common signs.

49. The Sun in the tenth degree of Libra, not conjoined with or aspected by a benefic, acts as a great liability.

50. Birth at midday raises one to a high position, as does birth at midnight, but in lesser measure. What is midday? Not necessarily twelve noon. The midpoint in time between sunrise and sunset is the local midday, and the mid-time between sunset and sunrise is local midnight. Allow a margin of twelve minutes on either side to mark the central zone of twenty-four minutes. Example: Sunrise at New Delhi on 1st January 1974 at 7:04 AM I.S.T. and sunset at 5:32 I.S.T. Local midnoon will therefore be at 12:17:30 PM or, rounding off, at 12:18 PM. The central noon zone will therefore be from 12:06 to 12:30 PM I.S.T. This rule, strictly speaking, does not fall within the scope of this book, because it does not involve a conjunction or aspect between planets, but being a conjunction of the Sun (the planet for position, power and prestige) with the Midheaven it confers high rank, especially if the Sun is conjoined with or aspected by benefics and the dispositor of the Sun is also well placed by sign and beneficially conjoined and/or aspected.

51. Apart from the Tenth house and the lord of the Tenth, there are four significators for rank and status: the Sun, Mercury, Jupiter and Saturn. Each of these planets well placed and beneficially conjoined and/or aspected contributes to a rise in position.

52. The lord of the Second in an angle conjoined with a benefic and an exalted planet in the Second and a benefic aspecting the Ninth house: Highly exalted position.

53. The lords of the First, Fourth and Ninth in the Tenth and the lord of the Tenth in the First aspected by a benefic: Same as in 52 above.

54. The lords of the First, Fourth and Tenth in the Tenth and the lord of the Tenth in the First or aspecting it: Same as in 52 above.

Thus we have given, in this chapter, 354 important combinations based on the conjunctions and aspects of planets.

10
JUDGMENT
GUIDELINES

THE FIRST PRINCIPLE to be kept in mind is that in Hindu astrology there is no weight attached to the factor of orb. Only in solar returns is the principle of orbs recognized, because that system was borrowed from Middle Eastern astrology, absorbed by the Hindus, and now flies the flag of Hindu astrology. On principle, an imported item may be as good as or even better than an indigenous one, and there should be no ethnocentric barriers against importing knowledge and know-how. In the matter of dress and dishes, medicine and merchandise, science and technology, how completely have we absorbed what was not Hindu in origin? And in the field of knowledge there are no political or geographical boundaries.

But what must be emphasized is that the principles enunciated by one school should not be haphazardly applied to another. And in the matter of conjunctions, any planets in the same sign, even if one is in the initial degree and the other at the very end of the sign, should be deemed to be together and therefore in conjunction. Similarly, planet 'A' in Aries will fully aspect planet 'B' in Libra regardless of the degrees occupied by 'A' and 'B' in Aries and Libra.

THE SECOND PRINCIPLE is that readers should regard each sign as a house (bhava) rather than thinking of signs and houses as different entities. The pitfall which confuses many students — and sometimes even scholars — is to regard the houses and signs as essentially different. The concept of the bhava or house in Hindu astrology determines which departments of life are to be judged from which signs. If Aries is rising, then Taurus constitutes the Second house, Gemini the Third and so on. Thus, those matters which are to be judged from the Second house are judged from Taurus, its lord, planets tenanting or aspecting Taurus, planets conjoined with or aspecting the lord of Taurus, etc. If Cancer is rising, Leo constitutes the Second house, Virgo the Third and so on. Thus the matters which we judge in regard to the Second house will be judged from Leo, its lord, planets tenanting or aspecting Leo, planets conjoined with or aspecting the lord of Leo, etc. This is the sole purpose of the concept of houses in Hindu astrology.

But as a result of the continuous influence of Middle Eastern astrology, many medieval authors of Hindu astrological works wrote learned treatises on house-division — notable among these are the *Shripati Paddhati* and the *Keshaviya Jataka Paddhati*, written by Shripati and Keshava respectively. They have introduced the system of ascertaining the meridian cusp, arriving at the distance between the ascending degree and the M.C., and trisecting it to fix the cusps of the Eleventh and Twelfth houses — in fact a variant of the system of house division known as Porphyry's to Western astrologers. Many modern scholars believe that a conjunction is in force if the two planets are in the same house, as determined above. Yet another school favors regarding the longitude of a particular planet as the cusp of the First house (in Hindu astrology the cusp is the midpoint of a house, rather than its beginning, as in Western astrology). Then, with the longitude of that planet constituting the First House cusp, the First house itself would be comprised of the fifteen degrees preceding and following that planet's position. Any planet which thus falls in the same house as the planet under consideration would be regarded as conjunct with it. Others say that for conjunctions and aspects the planets — for example planets 'A' and 'B' — should be placed one after the other on the cusp of the First house. Then draw lines of house demarcation as above from 'A', repeat the same experiment with 'B', and then determine their trines or squares, etc., and even their temporal relationships (friendship and enmity) on this basis.

Thus many in the astrological field have made attempts to refurbish the teaching of the old masters, each one according to his own notions, but in many cases have produced only hybrids of doubtful value.

We would, however, urge with all possible emphasis that one should forget all about the difference between signs and houses, and stick to the precept laid down by Varaha Mihira in the *Brihat Jataka,* Chapter 1, verse 4. He states: "The words *rashi, kshetra, griha, riksha, bha,* and *bhawan* all convey the same meaning." Literally, *rashi* means a sign, *kshetra* a field, *griha* a residential house, *riksha* a constellation, *bha* a constellation as well as a sign, and *bhawan* a mansion. The above authority, who flourished some two thousand years ago and whose text is still available (uncorrupted by dismemberment or interpolations, unlike Parashara's works, which, though old and authoritative, have been added to and amended to such an extent that it is difficult to separate the wheat from the chaff) has been quoted to reinforce the original concept that house computation in Hindu astrology was always considered in terms of signs rather than degrees. This should be followed in matters of conjunctions as well as aspects.

THE THIRD PRINCIPLE we would like our readers to keep in mind is that according to Kandala, another old master, the effect of a conjunction of two planets should be applied to their mutual full aspects as well. This is a broad rule, and exceptions must be allowed. For example, there will be a marked difference in effect between a Sun-Moon conjunction when the Moon's digital strength is zero and a Sun-Moon aspect when both are in the Seventh house from each other on a full Moon day when the Moon is strong. But the general principle is that planets, when conjunct, join their forces (which may be harmonious or otherwise according to their individual nature and characteristics, and therefore good or evil in the resultant effects), and that they do likewise through mutual full aspect upon each other. Thus Rudra Bhatta, on page 110 of his *Vivarana*[1] quotes an old astrological aphorism:

Apply the principles of aspects to conjunctions and of conjunctions to aspects.

Discriminating readers will observe that in the case of conjunction the two planets are in the same sign (and by implication in the same house), have the same dispositor, and receive the same aspects (if any) from other planets, but when there is a full aspect between two planets, say Saturn in Gemini and Mars in Pisces (Saturn will be in the fourth from Mars and Mars in the tenth from Saturn, thus casting full mutual aspect), the two planets will be in different signs and therefore in different houses, their dispositors will be different, and so will the aspects they might be receiving from other planets. Therefore, on general principle, how can the effects for a conjunction be the same as for a mutual full aspect? It is true that each conjunction and aspect must ultimately be assessed against the background of the complete nativity — the location and position of the planets, their lordships, their strength or weakness, the aspects they receive and cast, etc. — and that no textbook could possibly delineate all the potential permutations and combinations. It is due to one factor alone — the basic qualities of planets — that the ancient aphorism enunciates the principle that effects for conjunctions should be applied to aspects and vice-versa.

The assessment of a conjunction or aspect between two planets involves the appreciation of all the component factors. One should have a general background in astrology — the characteristics of signs, planets and houses, the individual effect a planet generates due to location in a

---

1   1926, Trivandrum edition.

particular sign or house, what affairs are judged from each of the twelve houses and the particular matters for which each planet is a significator. To describe all of these here would require space almost double the size of this book, and since these subjects have been dealt with exhaustively in our earlier book, *Hindu Predictive Astrology,* we recommend the above volume or any other standard work on the subject to those readers who are not already acquainted with it.

THE FOURTH PRINCIPLE is that when a planet, due to being too close to the Sun, is visible neither at night, after sunset, or before sunrise, it is called combust. In such a state a benefic loses part of its power to do good and a malefic becomes even more malignant. Generally, planets become combust at the following distances from the Sun:

The Moon within 12°

Mars within 17°

Mercury within 14° when direct and 12° when retrograde

Jupiter within 11°

Venus within 10° when direct and 15° when retrograde

Saturn within 15°

These are the normal distances. If a planet has a very wide latitude he will not become combust at the exact degree specified above, and in marginal cases the ephemeris must be consulted. It is relevant to add that, according to a Western writer:

Cazimi, in modern astrology, is when a planet is in what is called the heart of the Sun or within 17' of its body. It is said to fortify the planet as much as the combustion debilitates it.

Further, the same author adds:

It is said by Ptolemy that a planet, when combust, can neither save nor destroy, but it impregnates the Sun with its power, whether good or evil."[2]

Lilly's *Astrology* (a 17th century work) defines Cazimi as follows:

---

2   See *Anima Astrological Guide* by Bonatus, originally published in London in 1676.

The heart of the Sun, or being within 17 minutes exact longitude of the Sun, which is considered a strong position,

but Zadkiel comments that this view is erroneous. No such phenomenon is recognized in Hindu astrology. What is recognized, however, is that since Mercury and Venus are always near the Sun, not as much blemish is attached to them through combustion as to other planets.

So always scrutinize whether a planet is combust. If so, draw inferences in the light of the above. This applies not only to conjunctions but to the aspecting or aspected planet also. Rudra Bhatta states, on page 265 of his *Vivarana:*

An aspect by a planet who is himself in an enemy's sign or combust gives inauspicious results.

THE FIFTH PRINCIPLE is that when planets are retrograde, their power to do good or evil is enhanced. Thus benefics become more powerful to do good and malefics more malevolent to do evil. Mantreshwara, the illustrious author of the *Phala Deepika,* in Chapter 9, verse 20 of that work makes no distinction between benefics and malefics and states:

When a planet is retrograde in motion, he produces effects similar to those that would arise due to his occupying the sign of his exaltation, though the planet be in his enemy's sign or in debilitation.

The *Uttarakalamrita,* another old Sanskrit work, condemns a planet that is both in his sign of exaltation and retrograde. Chapter 2, verse 6 states:

When a planet is retrograde in motion, his strength is similar to that when in exaltation. If a planet is conjoined with a retrograde planet, his strength is half. If a planet be retrograde while in his sign of exaltation it is equivalent to debilitation. On the other hand, if a planet be in his debilitation and also retrograde, his strength is similar to that when in exaltation.

The *Saravali,* a much older and more standard work, states in Chapter 5, verse 14:

Some opine that if a planet is in his sign of exaltation and retrograde, he has no strength.

This by implication is not the author's own view but only a reference to views held by others. Light is thrown on his own views in the same chapter, verse 39, where he states:

Retrograde planets are very powerful; the *shubhas* (benefics) confer kingship while the *papas* (malefics) cause a lot of misery and aimless wandering.

Thus we have stated our view that it is good for benefics to be retrograde, but not for malefics. Please remember that the Sun and Moon are never retrograde, only the other five.

THE SIXTH PRINCIPLE is to note whether a planet is in his own sign, his sign of exaltation, or that of his debilitation. These relationships are detailed in the following table.

PLANET	OWN SIGN	EXALTATION	DEBILITATION
Sun	Leo	10° Aries	10° Libra
Moon	Cancer	03° Taurus	03° Scorpio
Mars	Aries & Scorpio	28° Capricorn	28° Cancer
Mercury	Gemini &Virgo	15° Virgo	15° Pisces
Jupiter	Sagittarius & Pisces	05° Cancer	05° Capricorn
Venus	Taurus & Libra	27° Pisces	27° Virgo
Saturn	Capricorn & Aquarius	20° Libra	20° Aries

Thus if there is a conjunction of the Moon and Jupiter in Cancer it will yield far better results than a conjunction of the same two planets in Capricorn, for in Cancer Jupiter will be in his sign of exaltation and the Moon in his own house, while in Capricorn Jupiter will be in debilitation and Moon will not be in an especially worthwhile location. The general rule is that any planet, whether benefic or malefic, yields very good results in exaltation or its own sign, while a planet in its sign of debilitation yields a very feeble measure of good if benefic and, if malefic, causes extremely bad effects.

THE SEVENTH PRINCIPLE is: If a planet is not in its own house, exaltation, or debilitation, note whether it is in a great friend's sign, a friend's, neutral's, enemy's or great enemy's sign.

And what do we mean by the words friends, neutrals and enemies in the context of astrology? There are two kinds of relationships in astrology. One is called natural, and holds good for all charts. It is as follows:

PLANET	FRIENDS	NEUTRALS	ENEMIES
Sun	Moon, Mars, Jupiter	Mercury	Venus, Saturn
Moon	Sun, Mercury	Mars, Jupiter, Venus, Saturn	None
Mars	Sun, Moon, Jupiter	Venus, Saturn	Mercury
Mercury	Sun, Venus	Mars, Jupiter, Saturn	Moon
Jupiter	Sun, Moon, Mars	Saturn	Mercury, Venus
Venus	Mercury, Saturn	Mars, Jupiter	Sun, Moon
Saturn	Mercury, Venus	Jupiter	Sun, Moon, Mars

Another kind of relationship is called temporal. This relationship changes from chart to chart. A special feature of temporal relationships which is different from the natural ones is that there are no neutrals — there is only friendship or enmity. Also, the relationship is mutual.

Let us explain. Look at the table of natural relationships. Mercury is the Sun's neutral but the Sun is Mercury's friend. Mercury is the Moon's friend but the Moon is Mercury's enemy. But in temporal relationship if A is B's friend then B is also A's friend, and if A is B's enemy then B is also A's enemy. How do we determine friendship and enmity in temporal relationships? Two planets in the same sign or in the second and twelfth, third and eleventh, or fourth and tenth from each other are deemed friends, while two planets in the fifth and ninth, sixth and eighth, and in opposite signs from each other are treated as enemies. Combining the results of the two sets, the resultant relationships are of five kinds:

1. A planet friendly both naturally and temporally is a great friend.

2. A temporal friend but natural neutral is a friend.

3. A friend in one system and an enemy in the other is a neutral.

4. A natural neutral but temporal enemy is an enemy.

5. An enemy in both systems is a great enemy.

A subtle distinction, however, is made in evaluating the two kinds of relationship — the natural one is given more weight than the temporal. Thus (a) a friend naturally but an enemy temporally and (b) an enemy naturally but a friend temporally will both, in the resultant relationship, be neutrals, but (a) is to be given more weight than (b) for the reasons already stated. The good a planet will do or is capable of doing will be at its maximum in (1) and at its minimum in (5) above in descending order, while the malefic influence a planet may generate or is capable of generating will be at a minimum in (1) and at a maximum in (5) in the ascending order. Thus with all conjunctions or aspects, examine whether a planet is in a great friend's, a friend's or in a great enemy's sign, etc.

THE EIGHTH PRINCIPLE is to take into account whether a planet is in its own, its exalted, debilitated, great friend's, friend's, neutral's, enemy's or great enemy's navamsha. What is a navamsha? The Sanskrit word means "one-ninth division." The ecliptic has 360°, divided into twelve signs of 30° each. Each sign constitutes 30° which, when divided by 9, yields 3° 20'. Thus each subdivision or navamsha of any sign has the following domains:

SUB-DIVISION	DEGREES
1.	00° 00' to 03° 20'
2.	03° 20' to 06° 40'
3.	06° 40' to 10° 00'
4.	10° 00' to 13° 20'
5.	13° 20' to 16° 40'
6.	16° 40' to 20° 00'
7.	20° 00' to 23° 20'
8.	23° 20' to 26° 40'
9.	26° 40' to 30° 00'

The subdivisions are allotted to the twelve signs in regular order so that:

SUB-DIVISION	ARIES, LEO, SAGITTARIUS	TAURUS, VIRGO, CAPRICORN	GEMINI, LIBRA, AQUARIUS	CANCER, SCORPIO, PISCES
1.	Aries	Capricorn	Libra	Cancer
2.	Taurus	Aquarius	Scorpio	Leo
3.	Gemini	Pisces	Sagittarius	Virgo
4.	Cancer	Aries	Capricorn	Libra
5.	Leo	Taurus	Aquarius	Scorpio
6.	Virgo	Gemini	Pisces	Sagittarius
7.	Libra	Cancer	Aries	Capricorn
8.	Scorpio	Leo	Taurus	Aquarius
9.	Sagittarius	Virgo	Gemini	Pisces

A peculiarity of Hindu astrology is the prime importance attached to a planet in a good navamsha. If the zodiacal sign corresponds to the body, the navamsha is the heart; if the sign is the tree, the navamsha is the fruit; if the sign is the car, the navamsha is the engine. A planet's location by navamsha has to be examined in the same way as its location by sign, explained earlier in regard to exaltation, rulership, debilitation, friendships and enmities, taking note of the concept that a planet which occupies the same sign in both the natal chart and navamsha — e.g. in the first navamsha (0° to 3° 20′) of Aries, Cancer, Libra and Capricorn, the middle navamsha (13° 20′ to 16° 40′) of Taurus, Leo, Scorpio and Aquarius, or the last navamsha (26° 40′ to 30°) of Gemini, Virgo, Sagittarius and Pisces — is considered very good. This position is called vargottama in Sanskrit. Hindu astrologers have placed it on a high pedestal. If this happens to be the exaltation, rulership or friendly sign of the planet, it is deemed very good and powerful; for example, the Sun in both the sign and navamsha of Aries or Leo. But even if a planet happens to be debilitated, for example Jupiter in Capricorn both by sign and navamsha, it is not deemed to be in such extremely bad straits, for much of its weakness is discounted due to the vargottama location.

THE NINTH PRINCIPLE is to note in which house a conjunction takes place, or in which houses the planets in aspect are positioned. The Sixth, Eighth and Twelfth are generally deemed evil houses, but malefics in the Third or Sixth are not condemned. Whether malefics or benefics, all planets are deemed good in the Eleventh. A malefic in its own sign is not deemed evil in any house, though in the Twelfth it would lead to heavy expenditure. For benefics the angles, trines and the Second house are deemed good positions, and a conjunction of benefics in these houses — especially in the First, Second and Eleventh, or a benefic in one of these houses aspected by a benefic from another good house — brings in much money. The Fourth, Seventh and Tenth houses are called angles (kendras in Sanskrit); the Fifth and Ninth are called trines (trikonas in Sanskrit). The First is an angle as well as a trine; the Sixth, Eighth and Twelfth are called trik (the three evil ones); the Third, Sixth, Tenth and Eleventh are called upachayas (a Sanskrit word indicating increase). Thus the Sixth house falls in two differing categories, trik (evil) and upachaya (good), and planets in the Sixth have to be carefully assessed in regard to the principles governing location. The placement of a planet in a particular sign or navamsha is referred to as *location,* whereas placement in the houses is called *position.* Astrologers therefore use the two terms "located in" or "posited in" to distinguish between two kinds of placement.

According to one school (see *Uttarakalamrita,* Chapter 4, verse 22), the lord of a trik (Sixth, Eighth or Twelfth) posited in another trik or one of the trik lords aspected by another trik lord is positively good if this placement, conjunction, or mutual aspect is unsullied by conjunction with or aspect from another planet. But we take this theory with a grain of salt.

When dealing with the conjunctions of planets, it is relevant to instruct those who are new to the subject that a conjunction of malefics not only spoils the house in which the malefics are posited, it also spoils the houses which are sixth, seventh, tenth and twelfth from it. A conjunction of benefics, on the other hand, not only does good to the house in which the conjunction takes place, but to the houses which are third, fourth, fifth, seventh, ninth, tenth and twelfth to it (see *Jataka Deshamarga,* Chapter 10, verses 31 and 35, and *Phala Deepika,* Chapter 15, verse 2).

THE TENTH PRINCIPLE, whether in regard to conjunctions or aspects, is to look to the planets' lordship of the houses. What do we understand by the term lord of a house? If Aries is the rising sign, then Mars is the lord of the First house; following Aries is Taurus, the lord of which is Venus, so Venus is the lord of the Second; next to Taurus is Gemini, so Mercury is the lord of the Third house and so on. If Capricorn is the Ascendant, then Saturn is the lord of the First house. Following Capricorn is Aquarius, so Saturn is the lord of the Second as well. Next to Aquarius is Pisces, so Jupiter is the lord of the Third house and so on.

Since the Sun and Moon are rulers of only one sign each, these two luminaries are lords of but one house. But Mars, Mercury, Jupiter, Venus, and Saturn each rule two signs, so each one of these is the lord of two houses in every nativity. It may be noted incidentally that the terms "ruler," "lord," and "owner" are all synonyms and convey the same meaning.

When the lords of good houses conjoin or aspect each other, it is always good. But when one planet which is the lord of a good house conjoins or aspects the lord of an evil one, the former does not remain entirely good and the latter is no longer entirely evil. As we have noted, one school of astrologers (see *Uttarakalamrita,* Chapter 4, verse 22) holds that it is good for the lord of an evil house to be conjoined with and/or aspected by the lord of another evil house — especially if the conjunction or one of the planets forming the aspect is actually in the Sixth, Eighth or Twelfth. But as we have said, we take this theory with a grain of salt.

1. The lord of the Eighth is considered the most evil, but exceptions to the rule are:

(a) If one and the same planet is lord of the First and Eighth, i.e. Mars for Aries Ascendant and Venus for Libra Ascendant, it is not considered evil.

(b) When one and the same planet is lord of the Fifth and the Eighth (i.e. Jupiter for Leo Ascendant and Mercury for Aquarius Ascendant) and posited in the Fifth or Eighth it is not evil.

(c) When one and the same planet is lord of the Eighth and Ninth (i.e. Saturn for Gemini Ascendant) and posited in the Ninth it is not evil.

2. The lord of the Sixth is considered evil, but the exceptions are:

(a) If the lord of the Sixth is in the Sixth.

(b) If one and the same planet is lord of the First and Sixth (i.e. Venus for Taurus Ascendant and Mars for Scorpio Ascendant) it is wholly auspicious if in the Ascendant; if it occupies any other house it is still rather good, though not entirely so.

(c) When one and the same planet is lord of the Sixth and Ninth (i.e. Jupiter for Leo Ascendant or Mercury for Capricorn Ascendant) it is good.

(d) When the same planet is lord of the Fifth and Sixth (i.e. Saturn for Virgo Ascendant) it is good if posited in Capricorn in the Fifth.

3. The lord of the Twelfth is also evil. The exceptions are:

(a) When it is also the lord of the Fifth (i.e. Venus for Gemini Ascendant and Mars for Sagittarius Ascendant) it is good.

(b) When it is also the lord of the Ninth (i.e. Jupiter for Aries Ascendant and Mercury for Libra Ascendant) it is auspicious.

(c) When it is also the lord of the First (i.e. Saturn for Aquarius Ascendant) and is posited in Aquarius in the First.

The *Uttarakalamrita* states, in Chapter 4, verse 9, that Jupiter as lord of the Third and Twelfth for Capricorn Ascendant is auspicious, but we think that despite Jupiter being a natural benefic, his beneficence is discounted when he rules the Sixth.

4. Regarding the lords of the good houses:

(a) The lords of the First, Fifth and Ninth are the best.

(b) Then come the lords of the Second, Fourth and Tenth.

(c) Then the lords of the Seventh, Eleventh and Third. Orthodox astrologers have not favored the lords of the Third and the Eleventh and have called them papas. They also state that the lords of the Seventh and Second are capable of causing death, but Mantreshwara, who, in Chapter 6, verse 32, has condemned the exchange of houses between the lord of the Third and the lord of any good house, himself states in Chapter 16, verse 7:

"If the lords of the Third house and the Ascendant be conjoined or mutually exchange places and be also strong, the native will be brave, chivalrous and helpful to his brothers. He achieves his target due to his innate courage." The conjunction of the lord of the Eleventh with the lord of a good house or a mutual aspect between them is conducive to good income. It is only when the lords of an angle and a trine combine that conjunction with or full aspect from the lord of the Third or Eleventh pulls down the native's position. And, barring a tendency to cause illness, the lords of the Second and Seventh are considered good. Therefore we have called these lords good.

5. When one and the same planet is the lord of both an angle and a trine he is exceptionally good (for Taurus and Libra Ascendants, Saturn; for Cancer and Leo Ascendants, Mars; for Capricorn and Aquarius Ascendants, Venus).

6. When the lords of the Second and Seventh houses conjoin (particularly in the Second or Seventh) or aspect each other, it is good for wealth but evil for health.

7. For office, authority, and position in life, a conjunction of the lord of an angle with the lord of a trine, or between lords of two or more angles with the lord of one or the lords of both trines is exceptionally good, provided the conjunction or mutual aspects between the lords of angle and trine are not combined with or aspected by the lords of the Third, Sixth, Eighth or Eleventh. Thus if the lords of the First and Tenth are together in the First or Tenth, or the lords of the Ninth and Tenth are together in the Ninth or Tenth, it is an excellent conjunction.

Parashara delineates special effects if the lords of two consecutive houses are conjoined:

First & Second	Gain of money
Second & Third	Government service
Third & Fourth	Commander of an army
Fourth & Fifth	Minister to a king
Fifth & Sixth	Perpetrates cruel acts
Sixth & Seventh	Good position
Seventh & Eighth	Death of spouse
Eighth & Ninth	Devaluation of good luck
Ninth & Tenth	Exalted position
Tenth & Eleventh	Gains a treasure trove
Eleventh & Twelfth	Loss of debts (i.e. freedom from debts)
Twelfth & First	Loss of money

Readers must not neglect the factor of house rulerships, and those who do so run the risk of arriving at incorrect inferences. For example, suppose we have to appraise a conjunction of the Moon, Mars and Jupiter, none of which are combust, and that the Moon has good digital strength. Let us say that they occupy particular degrees in Aries, so that the dispositor Mars is also strong in his own house. Let us say they are in good navamshas also. Now let us say that in one chart these three planets are in the First house: therefore the house of occupancy will also be good and the planets will be the lords of the First, Fourth, Eighth, Ninth and Twelfth. We have already mentioned that no blemish is attached to the lord of the Eighth when he is also the lord of the First; likewise Jupiter, due to ownership of the Ninth, is good despite its lordship of the Twelfth. So this is a beautiful conjunction of the lords of the First, Fourth and Ninth and will be an excellent proposition for good luck and prosperity (lord of the Ninth), real estate (lord of the Fourth) and accomplishments due to personal effort, initiative and courage (lord of the First).

Now let us say that in another chart this very conjunction is in the same sign and that the planets are in identical degrees but that they are all in the Twelfth house. The conjunction is of the same planets — the Moon, Mars and Jupiter — but the planets now occupy an evil house, i.e. the Twelfth. And we are now considering a conjunction of the lords of the Third, Seventh, Eighth, Eleventh and Twelfth. True, the Moon and Jupiter are natural benefics, but the lord of the Third in the Twelfth does not promote Third house affairs. True also, Jupiter is the lord of the Eleventh, the house of income and gains, but what good can he do when he is in the house of expenditure? The lord of the Seventh, Mars, though in his own sign Aries, connects the house of marriage and partnership (the Seventh) with the house of expenditure (the Twelfth). Such a conjunction would give little happiness, but be characterized by heavy expenses or even indebtedness as well as loss of strength and vitality, being the twelfth (expenditure) from the First (bodily stamina). It will easily be seen how we must bestow due regard to the lordship of houses.

This principle applies to aspects also. Jupiter, lord of the First and Tenth for Pisces Ascendant or lord of the First and Fourth for Sagittarius Ascendant, is wholly benefic naturally and through lordship. His aspect will be extremely good. But for Taurus Ascendant, Jupiter will be the lord of the Eighth and Eleventh, so how can his aspect generate the same good effects as in the former case? Let us illustrate the principle by reference to a natural malefic, say Mars. Mars as lord of the Fifth (trine) and tenth (angle) for Cancer Ascendant is a first-class planet due to his owning both a trine and angle, and if he aspects the Moon (lord of the First house for Cancer Ascendant) it will be a first-class aspect. But if Virgo is rising, Mars will be the lord of the Third and Eighth, and his aspect on the Moon will not be good — rather, due to lordship of the Eighth, he may cause distress and ill health.

In this way the effects of conjunctions and aspects must be determined and synthesized.

It is, however, relevant to add in this context that we should never ignore whether the planets conjoining or aspecting are natural benefics or malefics. Let us illustrate. Suppose Aries is the Ascendant. A conjunction of Mars and Saturn will be a conjunction of the lords of the First and Tenth, hence excellent. But suppose the two planets are conjunct in the Fifth house. This conjunction involving the lords of the First and the Tenth will be good for one's position in life but, in the Fifth house, it will spoil happiness in respect to children because the Fifth house governs children and because Mars and Saturn are natural malefics.

THE ELEVENTH PRINCIPLE is that one should never ignore the dispositors of planets in conjunction or aspect. Their strength or weakness by location, position and the aspects they receive also constitutes a factor. What is a dispositor? The dispositor is the lord of the sign in which a planet is located. For example, if Venus is in Capricorn, then the ruler of Capricorn, Saturn, is the dispositor of Venus.

Now suppose we have a conjunction of three planets in Gemini. To assess the influence generated by this conjunction, we have also to mark how its dispositor — Mercury, the lord of Gemini — is located, posited or aspected. Suppose Mercury is in debilitation in Pisces and also aspected by Saturn, a malefic. Planets in Gemini, even if inclined to do good, would do so in a poor way, and if inclined to do evil, the effects would be much worse. On the other hand, if the dispositor of the planets in Gemini, i.e. Mercury, is strong in Virgo in his sign of exaltation and also aspected by a strong Jupiter, then the planets in Gemini, if inclined to do good, would show excellent results and if inclined to do evil will be largely mitigated. So the dispositor must also be scrutinized; not only the dispositor of the sign, but the navamsha dispositor also. What is a navamsha dispositor? Suppose a planet is at 2° Gemini. Thus it is in Gemini sign, Libra navamsha. Mercury will be the dispositor by sign and Venus the navamsha dispositor. This applies not only to the dispositors and navamsha dispositors of planets in conjunction, but also when planets aspect each other.

Perhaps some readers may raise their eyebrows and surmise that we are stretching a point too far and going to the extent of hair-splitting when we recommend the appraisal of the dispositors of both the sign and the navamsha. To such critics, our only apology is that we are only walking in the steps of the old masters. The *Keshaviya Jataka*[3] (page 107, verse 5), an old and standard work, recommends the same. So does another Sanskrit work, the *Janma Patrika Vidhanamt,*[4] which, on page 6,1 advises computation of strength on the basis of the sign and navamsha dispositors. The *Jataka Deshamarga,* another standard Sanskrit work written a few centuries back in South India, states in Chapter 10, verse 17:

> If the dispositor of the navamsha in which the lord of a house is located is weak the effect is frustration, but if it be strong there is accomplishment of the affairs of the house under consideration.

Even Varaha Mihira, the doyen of Hindu astrologers, in *Brihat Jataka,* Chapter 10, verses 1 to 4, advises looking up the navamsha dispositor of the lord of the Tenth from the Ascendant, sun-sign and moon-sign, and predicts different shades of effects according to whether the said navamsha dispositors are in their own signs, a friend's or enemy's.

THE TWELFTH PRINCIPLE is that, when judging conjunctions, one must take into account whether the sign in which the planets are conjoined receives the aspect of benefics or malefics. Benefic aspects improve; the malefic ones do otherwise.

---

3   Bombay edition 1933.
4   Benares edition 1935.

This applies also to cases where one planet aspects another. Suppose the Moon is in Cancer and Venus aspects it. There will be a qualitative difference in the assessment of Venus' aspect on the Moon according to:

1. Whether or not Venus is conjoined with another planet (taking into account the quality of the planet conjoining)
2. Venus' lordship and position
3. Whether Venus receives the aspect of a benefic such as Jupiter or a malefic such as Saturn.

An ancient authority quoted in an old Sanskrit work states:

There is wealth due to conjunction with Jupiter and adversity due to that with Saturn. And when both features are present, there are mixed results.

What applies to conjunction applies by implication to aspects also. And while commenting on verse 18 in Chapter 16 of the *Hora Shastra,* Rudra Bhatta states that a planet aspected by his enemy gives inauspicious results. "This general overriding principle should always be borne in mind." Therefore, these principles have to be applied not only to the aspected planet but also the one making the aspect.

THE THIRTEENTH OVERRIDING PRINCIPLE is that readers should not be led away by one factor of a conjunction or aspect. It is the overall analysis and examination of the birth chart which affords the final clues. Just as one robin does not make the spring, so also one astrological feature alone does not raise a person to overlordship or doom him for life. The principles and precepts laid down by the old masters and applied to thousands of charts during our sixty-five years of practice (since 1927) have been succinctly stated in this chapter. They hold good not only for the evaluation of conjunctions and aspects but for general assessment also, because they form the 5foundations on which planetary evaluation is based. Let us illustrate. Suppose a particular conjunction or aspect in a chart indicates poverty. But if the lords of the First, Second and Eleventh are strong, the native — despite that unfortunate conjunction or aspect — may be very rich and own real estate if the Fourth house is strong, may be generally lucky and prosperous if the Ninth house is strong, and may lead a happy and luxurious life if the Moon, Venus and Jupiter are strong. Students must always take an overall or integrated approach.

✳ ✳ ✳

Astrology is an exact science but prediction a delicate art. No book, however encyclopedic, can cover all the possible permutations and combinations. Students will do well to apply the principles and draw conclusions after synthesizing the component factors. If they strictly follow the guidelines, they will be happily amazed at the accuracy of their findings.

BIODATA

PANDIT GOPESH KUMAR OJHA M.A., LL.B., son of Pandit Ramabhadra Ojha, M.A., LL.B., held degrees in Sanskrit and Law. The January 1966 issue of *Life Magazine* noted him as one of the best astrologers in the world. He was a great scholar and a pioneer in writing books on Vedic astrology, physiognomy, and palmistry (known as Samudrik Shastra), many of which are used as textbooks in India. He was honored with the title of Daivagya-Shiromani or "the crown jewel of those who know the future (astrologers)" and also the title of Jyotish-Kala-Nidhi by Swami Sivananda of the Yoga Vedanta Forest University, Rishikesh, India.

PANDIT ASHUTOSH OJHA B.A., M.A., the only son of Pandit Gopesh Kumar Ojha, began his study of astrology at the age of five. He comes from a family of astrologers whose astrological practice is traced back through six generations. He holds a degree in Mathematics and a Masters in English literature. For the past 25 years he has intensively taught and practiced astrology in 35 countries and written books on Vedic astrology, numerology, palmistry, and physiognomy.

VEDIC ASTROLOGY COMPUTER PROGRAM

PC-JYOTISH, a Vedic (Hindu) astrology computer program for IBM
compatable computers, is now available. Its features include:
- *South & North India chart styles*
- *Rasi (sign) and Bhava (house) charts*
- *Navamsa and other Varga (divisional) charts*
- *Shadbala*
- *Summary Tables — relationships & locations; Sign/house qualities & relationships*
- *Nakshatras — lords/sublords & pada lords*
- *Vimshopak*
- *Planetary Significators*
- *Ashtaka Varga — complete*
- *Vimshottari dashas, bhuktis & sub-bhuktis (365¼ or 360 days year)*
- *Pop-up Transit window with Ashtaka Varga & Nakshatra divisions*
- *Aspects Table*
- *Range of Ayanamshas or your own*
- *Easy to use, user driven program*
- *Mouse support*
- *Changing input data immediately alters on-screen tables & charts*
- *Pull-down menus*
- *Print to file or any ASCII printer*
- *Complete on-screen functions*
- *As many charts & tables on-screen as user desires*
- *User arranges windows on-screen*
- *Chart storage limited only by disk space*
- *Manual with glossary by David Frawley*
- *Program range: 1500 BC to 2200 AD*
- *Requires 420k ram*
- *Color/mono, hi-res mode — no graphics card required, and more*

DEMO program $5.00 (refunded if program purchased) plus shipping &
handling.

BOOKS OF RELATED INTEREST

The Astrology of the Seers
A Guide to Vedic Astrology by David Frawley
   ISBN 1-878423-05-3   342 pp. $18.95

Myths and Symbols of Vedic Astrology by Bepin Behari
   ISBN 1-878423-06-1   278 pp. $14.95

Fundamentals of Vedic Astrology
Vedic Astrologer's Handbook, Volume I by Bepin Behari
   ISBN 1-878423-09-6   254 pp. $14.95

Planets in the Signs and the Houses
Vedic Astrologer's Handbook, Volume II by Bepin Behari
   ISBN 1-878423-10-X apprx 275 pp. $14.95

Astrological Healing Gems by Shivaji Bhattacharjee
   ISBN 1-878423-07-X   128 pp. $7.95

Ayurvedic Healing
A Comprehensive Guide by David Frawley
   ISBN 1-87842 3-05-3   342 pp. $18.95

For more information call or write:

Passage Press
P.O. Box 21713
Salt Lake City, UT 84121-0713
(801) 942-1440